BLUNDERING

into

PARADISE

by

EDGAR DEWITT JONES

With an Introduction by

GAIUS GLENN ATKINS

1 9 3 2

Harper & Brothers Publishers

NEW YORK AND LONDON

Blundering into Paradise

To

My Uncle Beloved

HONORABLE H. H. RUMBLE

Contents

Introduction

A new volume of sermons by Edgar DeWitt Jones is an event for all good friends of good sermons, good literature—and Dr. Jones. Though it is by no means so widely recognized as it ought to be, a good sermon may be very good literature; indeed it is not likely to be a good sermon unless it is good literature. There is an amount of sound thinking and good writing touched by rare moral insight in the preaching of our own time which will strongly stand comparison with the preaching of any period and with the form and content of contemporaneous serious thinking and writing—whoever does it.

Dr. Jones' sermons belong to this elect company. He himself has ripened into the rare force and beauty of his maturity of style and message on a street which has seen in the last twenty years many preachers of distinction come—and go. The demands of Woodward Avenue, Detroit, are very searching. The man who meets and masters them has proved his power, his patience, and his grace. Edgar DeWitt Jones began with the rather modest church of a communion not strongly represented in Detroit. He has carried it for almost a decade and a half through many vicissitudes and seen it finally housed in Gothic loveliness, commanding in situation, influence, and strength. Those of us who know him best know through what wisdom of patience and faith this has been accomplished. His church is the creation of his gracious spirit and his wise and winning message.

His preaching is of its own kind. He is deeply saturated in great books and the critical lover of great men. His library is—in certain departments—unique, and some shelves of it would make any collector's mouth water. He is the disciple of the idealist in politics, the writers of lasting books, and the poets. His style has taken the qualities of this select fellowship, his message has been molded upon fundamental aspects of social and religious thought.

And he has kept it all richly human. There is a cumulative clarity in what he says, an allure of personality and discipline of delivery, which no book can quite suggest, in the way he says it, and a dearly-bought and sympathetic understanding of human ways and needs in the very texture of his message, which combine to make his preaching what it is.

Some of these sermons I have seen already in the publications of his church, others I have read in manuscript. They cover a wide range; they are telling in topic, original in approach, vital, soundly religious, and substantial in power. They are Jones at his best—the perpetuation and amplification of a voice whose music the stately arches of his church enrich but do not confuse. And for those of us who have known him long and cared for him so greatly the best thing about any sermons Dr. Jones preaches is just Jones himself. It is a happy chance to introduce to waiting readers a man of so many contacts, so many achievements and an always widening reputation, and to sign oneself his friend.

GAIUS GLENN ATKINS

Auburn Theological Seminary,
September 15, 1931.

BLUNDERING into PARADISE

The penitent robber came into his own not at the eleventh, but the twelfth hour. He literally blundered into Paradise. But for that matter, so do many of us. The divinity that shapes our ends is something more than poetry. This man who blundered into Paradise was both a wastrel and a wonder. However the wonderment is not on the manward side, but the Godward.

I

The story of the penitent robber and what happened to him in the hour of death is incomparably tender and beautiful. The world's masters of the short story—that most difficult of literary arts—De Maupassant, Edgar Allan Poe, O. Henry—never produced a story of such dramatic power or such surprising climax. As Sir William Robertson Nicoll said, "This story must be true, for it never could have been imagined."

The story appears in extraordinary brevity. Only eighty-five words are used to tell the tale. There are a few bold black strokes, a splash or two of color, and the picture is complete. We do not know the penitent's name, although tradition has supplied one. These robbers who died with Jesus were lawbreakers of Jerusalem and known to the police. Caught in some act of violence, they were arrested, tried, sentenced to die, and the sentence carried out. These men were two of a kind until a little while before the end. Then a change came over one of them: he rebuked his fellow robber, made a contrite confession of his sins, sought forgiveness and received it abundantly. This man lived as a sinner and died like a saint. He had not planned this wonderful thing. He blundered into Paradise.

> "Some may perchance, with strange surprise,
> Have blundered into Paradise.

3

In vast dusk of life abroad
They fondly thought to err from God,
Nor knew the circle that they trod;
And, wandering all the night about,
Found them at noon where they set out.
Death dawned, Heaven lay in prospect wide;—
Lo! They were standing by His side!"

Life is filled with experiences of unexpected awakenings of conscience and the discovery of God. To be sure, not so dramatic and unexpected as in the case of the penitent robber, but in essence the same. Think of Saul of Tarsus flinging himself against the young church, arresting the followers of Christ, consenting to Stephen's death, and in the midst of this bloody business suddenly brought face to face with a power that would not let him go. He met Christ on the Damascus way and nothing was ever the same again. He blundered into the greatest apostleship of the Christian era.

Recall that brilliant, beautiful, hot-blooded Numidian lad who at an early age gave himself to the world, the flesh, and the devil, bound himself down with the fetters of vicious habits. Think of this brilliant youth suddenly in the midst of his prodigal ways hearing the voice of God ringing in his ears like the strokes of some mighty bell. Thus it was that this young man, destined to be known as St. Augustine, was moved to open a manuscript at the place where St. Paul wrote, "Not in rioting and drunkenness, not in chambering and wantonness. But put ye on the Lord Jesus Christ, and make not provision for the flesh to fulfill the lust thereof." And lo! this bold young blunderer turned from his old ways, became an eminent Christian theologian, lived to write that lovely sentiment, "We were made for Thee, O Lord, and our souls find no rest until they rest in Thee." Augustine blundered into sainthood.

Is it not true that many of us stumbled in the dark upon *transit.* a door of hope, and, lo! the door opened into the way of peace and power? In the wild deserts of desire we blundered our way across hot sands only to find an oasis of spiritual strength when we least expected it; at the very point where it seemed that the springs of the spirit were dry, lo! there was a brook that bubbled up into life eternal. In the midst of some crisis we plunged into chaos only to emerge into an orderliness that astonished us.

A great deal of life is blundering on our part. Life *Proposition* is not as simple as some would have us believe. It is sufficiently complex to bewilder us and becomes more so with the passing years. We do not move forward on straight lines, although we start out that way often, but by zigzag paths. If our careers could be traced by lines, those lines would perforce be often broken. At times they would form right angles; some of the lines would be crooked, others curves and even circles. How blindly we blunder our way through this life, and how strangely a Power meets us even in our blunderings and helps to salvage the best out of wreck and apparent ruin!

> "There's a divinity that shapes our ends,
> Rough hew them how we will."

This story of the penitent who blundered into Paradise *I.* is an eloquent reminder of the truth that God is everywhere. This is a primary lesson that religion endeavors to teach—the gospel of the everywhereness of God. When a man actually believes that God is everywhere, he has come a long way in his religious life. Unfaith loses God in the vastness of the universe. Scepticism feels for Him

5

vaguely. Feeble faith gropes after Him falteringly. Atheism finds Him nowhere. Yet God is never far from His children. He is the unescapable God.

The aim of worship is to sharpen the sense of the worshiper so that he may know that God is everywhere, not merely in one place—the church, temple, sanctuary. The ancient Jews believed that Jehovah was present in the Temple at Jerusalem in a particular sense, but even so they came to believe that He was not confined to the Holy of Holies. Jesus took an immense stride forward when in His conversation with the woman of Samaria He declared that God is a spirit and they who worship Him must worship Him in spirit and in truth. Such spiritual worship may be and frequently is apart from special places, yet I suppose the church, temple, sanctuary will always hold a unique place in the devotional life. Nobody short of a fool would say that learning is confined to a college, for it is not. Yet the school and college inspire a love of learning, and a church building, a period of worship employing eloquent symbols, may greatly enlarge and deepen the sense of God's presence.

Another assurance in this amazing story is that God is closest to His children when He seems farthest away. Job thought himself cast off of God as he sat in the midst of his misery, tormented by his so-called comforters, and stripped of all his earthly possessions. Yet it was in that experience that he found a new meaning in God, a new assurance that He is and that He is a rewarder of them that seek after Him. It was not merely a clever literary device that God should speak to Job out of the storm. He speaks to us in time of storm. The penitent robber went on his way of wrong-doing apparently abandoned of God, and indeed had turned his back upon Him, so far as out-

6

ward appearances are concerned. From a prison he was led to the place of execution, nailed to the upright beam alongside of One upon the central cross, to the natural eye as helpless as himself. Gradually he saw life differently because he saw it in the light of Jesus dying there by his side. What a flood of light poured upon things as perceived from that central cross. The penitent rebuked his fellow robber, who raged violently and brutally against the dying Galilean. The penitent one acknowledged the uniqueness of Jesus, asked to be remembered when he came into his kingdom, and was rewarded by the surprising words, "Today shalt thou be with me in Paradise." In the darkest hour of that robber's existence he saw a light. Lo! God was by his side!

How true it is that in a brief space of time, almost in an instant, one may see life differently, see oneself as one really is, and see God as never before. I have been greatly interested in reading an account of a young soldier named Frederick L. Collins, who narrowly escaped death in an airplane, and what happened to him—I mean his way of thinking. He went up that day a selfish man, wholly devoted to his own interests, a thoroughgoing materialist. Then he looked death in the face and something happened to him. He saw God, felt God. Here is part of his own story:

"I never will know what happened to the plane. But somewhere, in the last two hundred feet, the gallant boy in the pilot's seat, wrestling silently with the stops and levers on the board in front of him, managed to gain a partial momentary control over the crippled craft. He swerved—oh, so little!—to the right. And slid, rather than fell, into a boggy marshland in the middle of the River Meuse.

"The ship was wrecked. So were some badly shaken nerves. But as far as I was concerned nothing mattered so much as the almost unbelievable thing that had happened to me during the sixty seconds I was so gloriously dead.

"I could never fear death again. At a distance of several years—even of several miles—it had been a terrifying thing. But when it came right up to us and touched me on the shoulder it wasn't at all unfriendly. It didn't hurt me. It changed me. My brain acted as it never had acted. My heart responded as it never had responded. My soul—for now I knew that I had a soul—rose to meet a Force which my eyes had never seen and my hands had never touched.

"How did I know that I had a soul?

"How do you know that you have hearing, sight? By using them. And for the first time I was using my soul.

"How did I know there was a Force?

"How do you know there is faith, love? By experiencing them. And for the first time I was experiencing God.

"Maybe—I don't know; it's only just supposing—but maybe heaven is like that!"

It would be interesting to know how it came about that of the two robbers who hung upon either side of Jesus, only one was affected by what he saw and heard from the central cross. Here were two men, both blunderers, lawbreakers, criminals. One of them calloused to any appeal to the spirit, blunderingly plunged into deepening darkness; the other, touched by the spirit and speech of Jesus, saw in him some representative of a higher life and was filled with a vast desire to be with him in the experience that lay beyond death, and so blundered into Paradise. How shall we account for the difference between these two companions of the cross?

8

If we knew their early lives perhaps we might understand it. Way back somewhere there must have been religious experiences in the penitent's past. David Smith, in a sermon on the perseverance of the saints, has a touching reference to the death of wicked old Jack Falstaff. Dame Quickly, who was with him when he died, tells of his nose becoming sharp as a penknife and describes his plucking at the coverlets of the bed, and she says "he babbled of green fields and running brooks." Dr. Smith thinks that Falstaff was thinking of the twenty-third Psalm, a memory of his boyhood days, and that this memory came to bless him in his dying hours across all the years of his ribald and sensual career. It may be so. And it may be that the penitent was penitent because he had, somewhere along the way, a religious experience, some sort of faith that left a little soil that would some day sprout a seed. At any rate, we may be sure that whatever the reason why one of those robbers repented and the other did not was due not to any unwillingness of Christ to pardon, forgive, receive. The difference was due to the dispositions, the will faculty of the two men, and back of these—environment, training, heredity, were involved.

If one could be sure that in the hour of emergency his eyes would be opened to see, and his ears to hear, spiritual truth, it would be an immense satisfaction since there can be no doubt that God is a God who will not let us go. He will not leave us. He will seek us out, but shall our eyes recognize Him? Shall our ears hear His voice? It is an inspiriting thought, and very full of comfort, that God is everywhere and that even our sins and blunderings do not drive Him away. It is a dreadful thought that the spiritual life can be so dwarfed and starved that the faculties for perceiving God and laying hold of Him can

9

become weakened, atrophied, to the point of moral paralysis.

This man who blundered into Paradise was both a wastrel and a wonder. He missed much that he might have had in life. He won everything in death but could not retrieve the past years. Better it is to do one's blundering soon instead of late; to find one's way to self-mastery and the good life before "the years draw nigh when thou shalt say, I have no pleasure in them." Better it is to be as a tree planted by the rivers of water that "bringeth forth its fruit in season," than "a brand plucked from the burning." All the same, the New Testament fact that one man could blunder into Paradise at the twelfth hour is amazing, not so much on the manward side, but surpassing wonderful on the Godward side.

CHRISTIANITY and COMMON HONESTY

> *The Bible from first to last puts a premium on honesty, truth-telling, justice. Jesus taught His followers to think righteously. The early Church abhored falsehood, crooked dealings. How fares modern Christianity and truth, honesty, justice? What has War done to the Sermon on the Mount?*

II

"No man can serve two masters; for either he will hate the one and love the other; or else he will hold to one and despise the other. Ye cannot serve God and mammon."

Matthew VI:24

"All things, therefore, whatsoever ye would that men should do unto you, even so do ye also to them; for this is the law and the prophets."

Matthew VII:12

"Ye therefore shall be perfect, as your heavenly Father is perfect."

Matthew V:48

What is the most perplexing problem in connection with Christianity? Is it miracles? I think not. Is it some doctrine supposed to be basic, the acceptance of which seems to stultify the intellect? I do not think so. Is it the problem of pain and suffering and the attempt to reconcile these with a Christ-like God? No, deep as this difficulty is, I do not think it is the deepest. The most perplexing problem of Christianity is the discrepancy between the ideals of its Founder and the practice of His followers.

Christianity is nearly two thousand years old. Its adherents number hundreds of millions. Its organized life is impressively large. Its buildings and equipment are both costly and numerous. Yet much of the so-called Christian world is still Pagan in outlook and customs. Physical force still rules the world to a larger degree than we like to confess. There is a suspicion, too, and widely entertained, that the teachings of Jesus, while beautiful, are visionary and impractical.

There are at least three reactions of humanity to the discrepancy between Christian ideals and practice, to wit, atheism, fanaticism, and institutionalism. Atheism is sometimes the last resort of a baffled believer who, unable to reconcile reason and faith, abandons his belief in God. Fanaticism takes the other horn of the dilemma and, mistrusting man coöperating with God, rests its case upon a miracle-working Deity who through some supernatural way will impose His will upon mankind and so usher in the happy consummation. Institutionalism is that view of life where one buries his idealism in organization, satisfies his soul with statistics, and ceases to worry over the failure of Christian teaching to captivate and transfigure society.

I concede that it is not practicable to draw straight lines between these groups or classifications. There is so much faith in the most sceptical and so much unbelief in the most orthodox, that it doesn't become any of us to stigmatize the rest of us. If just now I seem to be doing this very thing, God forgive me. I am trying to account for the discrepancy between Christian ideals and practice and the manner in which men and women react to the same.

Is Christianity practicable? Is the Sermon on the Mount to be taken seriously? There are some Christians who think so, evidently. There are those who tell us that the immediate practice of Jesus' teaching in that sermon is unthinkable, and that not until the millennium is an accomplished fact can the Sermon on the Mount be practiced. Still others, professing the Christian faith, do not worry themselves at all about this Sermon on the Mount. Alas! They disregard it wholly or view it in a detached manner.

Take a good look at the third Scripture just cited, "Ye,

therefore, shall be perfect, even as your heavenly Father is perfect." Does this seem visionary and impracticable? Maybe we have misunderstood it. The idea here is not that we are to be as perfect as our Father, but to be perfect as our Father in heaven is perfect. "We are not asked to be as good as God is, but we are commanded to be good as God is good, in the way that He is good. How is God good? The Sermon on the Mount is Jesus' simplest answer to that question. The Divine goodness differs from the goodness of the Philistine world not in its degree, but in its kind. The Philistine world loves its neighbors and hates its enemies. But the Eternal Goodness loves its enemies, blesses those that curse it, does good to those that hate it, and prays for those that persecute it. It makes its sun rise on the evil and on the good and sends its rain on the just and on the unjust. God differs from us morally, not because He knows more neighbors to love than we know, not because He has more enemies to hate than we have. His perfection is not a matter of degree at all. It is a matter of disposition, of quality. The Divine Goodness needs but one enemy to occasion its perfection, one persecutor to show its unlikeness to our imperfect goodness. Loving a thousand enemies would not make it any more perfect than loving one. Praying for a thousand persecutors would not enhance the qualitative perfection revealed in the prayer for one persecutor."*

What has all this to do with Christianity and common honesty? Very much, I venture to say, and in many ways, as may appear presently.

"An honest man's the noblest work of God." This is not a Biblical quotation. It is from the English poet, Alexander

* Willard L. Sperry.

15

Pope, but the idea expressed is thoroughly Biblical. From Genesis to Revelation the Bible puts a premium on honesty. Integrity is a basic virtue; truthfulness, a cardinal grace or quality. Anyone who supposes that the law of Moses is concerned mostly with ceremonies and rites is badly mistaken. There are ethical standards there high and holy; honesty is exalted and praised. In the Book of Psalms there is a selection devoted wholly to the praise of the ideal citizen. He is described minutely.

> "Lord, who shall sojourn in thy tabernacle?
> Who shall dwell in thy holy hill?
> He that walketh uprightly, and worketh righteousness,
> And speaketh truth in his heart;
> He that slandereth not with his tongue,
> Nor doeth evil to his friend,
> Nor taketh up a reproach against his neighbor;
> In whose eyes a reprobate is despised,
> But who honoreth them that fear the Lord;
> He that sweareth to his own hurt, and changeth not;
> He that putteth not out his money to interest,
> Nor taketh reward against the innocent.
> He that doeth these things shall never be moved."

The Proverbs of the Old Testament are filled with protest against dishonesty and the lying tongue. "A just balance and scales are the Lord's." . . . "A false balance is an abomination to the Lord." . . . "Lying lips are an abomination unto the Lord, but a lying tongue is but for a moment." . . . The prophets of Israel over and over again exalt righteousness, justice, and denounce falsehood, dishonesty, and crooked dealings.

Then came Jesus, who, building upon the foundation of Old Testament ethical teachings, raised the superstructure higher. In truth, he laid the foundations deeper down. He began with the thought instead of the deed, and illustrated in his own life the power of integrity, the influence of truth, the deathlessness of a character transparent in sincerity. He *could* say, "I am the truth"; he *could* say, "I am the way"; he *could* say, "I am the life." Jesus was never cynical; never lost faith in the possibilities of human goodness. He was hard on hypocrites, but exceedingly tender in his dealing with blundering humanity. He carried ever with him the atmosphere of moral strength, and a certain wholesome optimism.

Contrast with the spirit of Jesus as expressed, say, in the Sermon on the Mount, or in his personal relations with the Twelve, the publicans, and the sinners; the cynicism of this excerpt from the last will and testament of a Wall Street man—a will actually offered for probate in the State of New York:

"To my wife, I leave her lover and the knowledge that I wasn't the fool she thought I was.

"To my son, I leave the pleasure of earning a living. For thirty-five years he has thought that the pleasure was all mine. He was mistaken.

"To my daughter, I leave $100,000. She will need it. The only good piece of business her husband ever did was to marry her.

"To my valet, I leave the clothes that he has been stealing from me regularly for the last ten years. Also my fur coat that he wore last winter when I was in Palm Beach.

"To my chauffeur, I leave my cars. He has almost ruined them and I want him to have the satisfaction of finishing the job.

"To my partner, I leave the suggestion that he take some other clever man in with him at once if he expects to do any business."

The best answer to the clever cynicism of our day as exemplified in the writings of a Henry L. Mencken or a Sinclair Lewis, the caustic and often well-directed criticism of a Walter Lippmann, is a revival of common honesty in all the churches, an emphasis on integrity, a premium on rectitude. In the days when the young church was finding itself and seeking to promulgate the spirit and principles of Jesus, a flagrant case of dishonesty on the part of Ananias and Sapphira produced a tragedy in the congregational life of first-century Christians and left an impression that was ineradicable. The term "simony" owes its origin to an incident of early Christian history, when the gift of spiritual power was shown to be unpurchasable and the would-be buyer stigmatized unto the hour of his repentance.

The difficulty of practicing the principles of Christianity is not due solely to the individual, and whatever remissness or recreancy may be his, part of the difficulty is, that there is no wholly Christian society as yet, no general application of Jesus' teachings to community and national life. Much of the so-called Christian world is still anti-Christian in many of its systems, customs, and practices. Take the one fundamental issue of war, which is still accepted and resorted to by Christian nations, although lately "outlawed" on paper. War cannot be conducted without duplicity, lies, slander. The night before Woodrow Wilson made his address to Congress, taking us into the World War, he, in conference with Frank Cobb, editor of the *New York World*, spoke his heart. As a student of history he said he knew what it meant to take the nation into war. Then he added, "From now on we shall not be able to tell the truth." And, of course, it turned out as he predicted. We know now that the German atrocities were not true, that they were deliberately fabricated in order to awaken an intense hatred, without which successful wars cannot be fought.

Every nation lied about its enemy nations, deliberately, methodically lied. I, a minister of the Gospel, had a part in propagating falsehood during the period we were at war. I believed it to be the truth, of course. I was sent in the spring of 1918 to make a speech in a Mennonite community. The Mennonites are "conscientious objectors" and were lukewarm to the war spirit that swept over our country in 1917-18. I was accompanied by several veterans of other wars and the occasion was made a military holiday by the town in central Illinois where the meeting was held. There were flaunting flags and emblazoned banners. The school children sang patriotic songs. I felt the thrill of it all and believed that I was serving the cause of liberty and justice when in my speech I gave some account of the atrocities which had been described to me. I felt every word that I said, and as I talked I felt the hot blood coursing through my veins and heating my cheeks. At the time I never suspected that I was bearing false witness and making it easier for men to lie and for dishonesty to flourish in the years to come. I remember at this particular meeting one of my auditors was an old Mennonite farmer of childlike countenance, who looked up at me from the depths of his mild blue eyes as if to say, not bitterly, but in a mood of sad surprise, "And you, a minister of the Gospel of Jesus Christ, believe in war."

Now I shall have to confess that I am naturally a militarist. The trappings and tinsel of military life fascinate me. Long lines of marching men and martial music stir me "like the tap of a drum." Many a time my eye has danced to see the old flag in the sky. The traditions of my country are precious to me beyond words. Yes, naturally I am a militarist, but intellectually and spiritually I am anti-militaristic. I know what war does to the finer instincts of humanity, the elemental passions that it fires, the poison of hate it creates and releases. I know that war is contrary to both the letter and the spirit of the Christian religion, and I hold that nothing is more difficult or more desirable than to redeem patriotism from the evil of "jingoism."

It is a dreadful thing to subsidize the ministry of Christ's church to spread the propaganda of war and feed the fires of hate. One of the most famous of American preachers, it will be remembered, gave of his brilliant talents and immense influence to exploit the German atrocities before vast audiences in this country the fall and winter of 1917-18. The posters that announced his coming pictured him in gown and divinity hood against a background of burning villages and barbaric invasions. I heard this gifted minister on this subject twice, and once I sat near him at the speakers' table and examined certain evidences of German barbarity, among others the medal that the German government was said to have had struck in commemoration of the event of the sinking of the *Lusitania*, since proved to be a very clever and effective piece of anti-German propaganda. Although under the spell of the war spirit myself at that time, and willing to take my share of the opprobrium that has come upon us all who from the pulpit contributed to the atmosphere of poison, I felt the incongruity and sensed the shame of it, that so great a preacher of Christ, and one so highly honored, should be used for the exploitation of the very thing that Christianity condemns.

Yet it is not a surprising thing that when a nation goes

to war it carries irresistibly the vast majority of its citizens, including the churches and the ministers. There is a terrific conflict of loyalties at stake; to paraphrase nurse Edith Cavell, patriotism, for the time being, seems "enough" and to spare. "Like people like priest" is more often true than "like priest like people," and there is a reason. It is difficult for a teacher of the Christian religion to attempt to educate his hearers for peace when the agencies of the state are still busy educating the people for war. As long as war lasts, and we have education for war and immense preparations for war, peace on earth will be difficult, and the precepts of Christianity hard to practice. Every war is followed by a lowering of ethical ideals; liberalism wanes, progressive thought is halted and penalized. Out of war comes the organization of those who have participated, and inevitably, although sometimes unconsciously, such organizations perpetuate the spirit of war and make the path to peace more tortuous and difficult. Such an episode as the Teapot Dome scandal could not have happened in the years preceding the Great War without arousing the conscience of the American people to a white heat. Scandals follow in the wake of war because the public conscience has been dulled, ideals lowered and compromised, standards accepted that give the lie to the principles taught and practiced by Jesus.

Must it always be so? I think of those strange lines found in the pocket of an English soldier killed in action:

"Suddenly one day
The last ill shall fall away,
The last little beastliness that is in our blood
Shall drop from us as the sheath drops the bud,
And the great spirit of man shall struggle through
And spread huge branches underneath the blue.

In any mirror, be it bright or dim,
Man will see God, staring back at him."

That the practice of the precepts of Christ is difficult in a day like ours is all the more reason why we should keep the banner of idealism flying. The discussions and controversies in our churches ought not to be over doctrine wholly, but over deeds instead; not over ceremonies, but about character. The life of Christian people should be higher, finer, cleaner. We must be honest with one another; honest with our obligation to the church, the state, the home; and above all, honest with ourselves.

"An honest man's the noblest work of God." This land we love produced a great character who in addition to his other gifts was as ruggedly honest as the granite cliffs of the Rockies. In the year 1809 there were anxiety and expectancy in a log cabin in the backwoods of Kentucky, and on the twelfth day of February there was born a man child in that home. His parents were poor, respectable, and devoutly religious. The first sounds that fell upon the child's ears were the blow of a woodsman's ax and the call of the wild fowl. He grew up with certain ideals of truth and honesty, this backwoods boy, tall and gaunt, and in the timberlands of his Indiana home, amid humble surroundings, he began to manifest those ideals which led him on like some bright, particular star to the end. Over in Illinois, in the region of New Salem, he clerked in a store, and once when he overcharged a woman six and one quarter cents he carried the change to her after closing hours that same day, making a trip of several miles, all because his conscience was sensitive. Once when he was waiting on several customers he gave one of them a short weight, by mistake, of course. And when he discovered it he tied up the four ounces of tea due this customer and walked a long distance to her home and back again that he might go to bed with a conscience void of offense. He carried this same sensitiveness into the life of a practicing lawyer, carried it also into politics, carried it with him into the awful struggle to preserve the Federal Union, and, dying tragically, his life an offering for peace and unity, he gave to the world a memory of a life in which honesty was so conspicuous that his countrymen called him "Honest Abe."

Abraham Lincoln was not a member of any church, but he was naturally religious, and as he grew older the spirit of Christ took possession of him. He was a man of prayer and intimately acquainted with the Bible. He was an attendant on church services, but his intellectual honesty was such that he could not subscribe to some of the creeds, and when asked his reason for not uniting with the church he replied, "If any church will write on its altar as the sole condition of membership the words of Jesus, 'Thou shalt love the Lord thy God with all thy heart, and with all thy soul, and with all thy strength, and with all thy mind, and thy neighbor as thyself,' that church will I join." To be sure, those words are written on the altars of our churches, but there is so much else written there that is less important and non-essential, that this great affirmation of real religion is often obscured and sometimes hidden.

"No man can serve two masters; for either he will hate the one, and love the other; or else he will hold to one, and despise the other. Ye cannot serve God and mammon."

"All things therefore whatsoever ye would that men should do unto you, even so do ye also unto them: for this is the law and the prophets."

"Ye therefore shall be perfect, as your heavenly Father is perfect."

Mr. H. L. Mencken to the author:

DEAR DR. JONES:

Thanks very much for your pleasant note, and for the enclosure. Your apologia for your services to democracy during the great crusade is excellently done. I often wonder what will happen the next time the band begins to play. My fear is that many of the pacifists of today will leap to the barricades again.

My feeling is that the revival of common honesty that you preach is psychologically impossible. For some reason that appears to strike deeply into the character of the American people; they are always suspicious of frankness. The people they most admire are almost unanimously frauds. This, at all events, is my belief after thirty years of close observation.

Sincerely yours,

H. L. MENCKEN[1]

[1] This letter from Mr. Mencken was in answer to a note from me inclosing a copy of this sermon. It is printed here with his permission. —E. D. W. J.

"NEVER MAN SO SPAKE"

The Gospel narratives bear witness to the attraction of Jesus as a speaker. The multitudes hung enraptured on his utterances. Even his enemies conceded the charm of his speech. In what did this charm consist? Was it rhetoric, oratory, eloquence? Or does the secret of Christ's speech lie deeper than voice, personality, charm of words?

III

Imagine listening to a speech by Daniel Webster! Lo! his commanding form, brow of Jove, eyes glowing like an anthracite furnace, voice of melodious ease—think of hearing him in an oration or before a jury! What a memorable experience to have heard Webster in his famous reply to Senator Hayne when he closed with that phrase which has since become one of the nation's finest maxims, "Liberty and union, now and forever, one and inseparable."

Fancy sitting entranced under the golden speech of Henry Clay. In my college days in Transylvania, Lexington, Kentucky, I talked with an elderly woman who had heard him when she was a little girl. She spoke of the charm of his presence, the glow that suffused his face, the melting eloquence that fell from his lips. "Mr. Clay looked and spoke like a god," the old lady said. A few abide with us still who heard the famous Lincoln-Douglas debates. They speak of Mr. Lincoln's clear logic, the vigor of his thought, the quaintness of his stories, the lasting memory of his deep sincerity. Think of hearing Lincoln in that historic speech of four minutes at Gettysburg.

What an epochal experience to have heard St. Paul, a prisoner of the Lord, in his speech before King Herod Agrippa, when with becoming courtesy he began his speech saying: "I think myself happy King Agrippa, that I am to make my defense before thee this day, touching all the things whereof I am accused by the Jews; especially because thou art expert in all customs and questions which

27

are among the Jews: Wherefore I beseech thee to hear me patiently."

And supremely think of listening to the speech of Jesus of Nazareth! Fancy hearing him speak from his pulpit on the mountain-side, telling the parable by the seashore, reasoning with the Jews in the Temple, conversing leisurely in the home of Mary, Martha, and Lazarus, or talking amid the tender intimacies of the upper room in Jerusalem. Would it not be a day of precious memory—the day we heard Jesus talk of the Kingdom of God, discourse on the heavenly Father's love, interpret the Scriptures?

There are a number of references in the New Testament that bear upon the charm of Jesus' speech. When he returned to Nazareth and spoke in the synagogue, there it is chronicled that "All bear him witness and wondered at the words of grace which proceeded out of his mouth. And they said, 'Is not this Joseph's son?'" The people hung on his utterances. They said he spoke with authority. When certain officers were sent to arrest him they returned to the chief priests and Pharisees without him, and when chided for their failure to put him under arrest, those officers answered, "Never man so spake." That is to say, there was something in his very speech that entranced and awed them, made them favorably disposed to him despite their orders to take him prisoner. Then there is another significant allusion to the persuasive speech of Jesus. It is reported by Mark that the "common people heard him gladly." Surely, during the year of his popularity the crowds thronged about him that they might listen to his speech. Mary sat at his feet, forgetful of all else save that the Master was present, and the room was filled with the music of his speech.

28

In what did the charm of Jesus' speech consist? Was it his rhetoric, the choice of words, felicitous phrasings, pleasing allusions, delightful stories? Was it merely his oratory that led the people so to marvel at the graciousness of his speech? Are we to account for Jesus' power over the people on the basis of his eloquence? Now there is every reason to believe that he was a captivating speaker. His personality must have been strong, gracious, and magnetic. He was an out-of-door man, and we have no reference to his ever having been sick. He was accustomed to speak out in the open, and must have had a strong voice without any harshness or roughness of quality—a voice that arrested attention and won a hearing even among opponents. There is, I think, every reason to believe that Jesus was a magnetic and attractive speaker, but we cannot account for the power of his speaking solely on the ground of winsomeness, rhetoric, or any other impressive quality or style of speech.

When the officers reported that "Never man spake as Jesus," they surely did not have in mind his oratory. We may be reasonably certain that the common people did not hear him gladly solely because of his eloquence. There were reasons for his popularity more basic and far-reaching than those. The common people heard him gladly because he was saying something worth saying—something that had in it hope for the oppressed, courage for the fearful, comfort for the grief-stricken, health for the sick and ailing, redemption for the lost. Moreover, what he said and what he was were one and the same. This of itself signifies much. Said William Penn, quaintly, "There is a truth and beauty in rhetoric; but it oftener serves ill turns than good ones." Speech by and of itself, however golden, is incomplete until it is translated into deeds.

There is a story that appears from time to time involving two of the mighty personalities who adorned the last half of the nineteenth century in American history, Wendell Phillips and Henry Ward Beecher. Phillips was an aristocrat by birth, a blue-blooded Bostonian, and a most gifted and polished gentleman. He gave himself heart and soul to the cause of abolition and became the trumpet-toned agitator of that cause. Beecher was the greatest preacher of his generation and, all things considered, one of the greatest preachers Christianity has produced. He too was a friend of the slave. He too was a champion of the weak and the oppressed. These two men passed through a generation of agitation, of long and arduous campaigning in behalf of unpopular causes, and they lived to see the triumph of freedom. Following the heat and the labor of that period, both Beecher and Phillips entered upon a less tempestuous time, but they continued to lecture on various subjects, and always with appreciative hearers. One night it chanced that the two were in Chicago the same night, and Phillips was announced for a lecture. Beecher went to hear him. For an hour and a half Phillips poured out a limpid stream of eloquence, bright, brilliant, and informative. After the lecture the two famous orators went to Phillips' room in a near-by hotel. The Bostonian stretched himself out on a couch while Beecher paced back and forth, apparently under some stress of emotion. By and by he stopped by the couch on which his friend lay and in a voice of deepest concern inquired: "What's the matter, Wendell? Why is it you weren't yourself tonight? What's the matter?" Phillips sighed. "I know it, Henry. I know it. It was only a speech. I was not fighting for any needy cause; I was not defending any great truth. It was just words, words, words."

30

Yes, both public and private speech may be merely "words, words, words," but the speech of Jesus of Nazareth was more than rhetoric, more than any mere charm of personality. The words he spoke, they were spirit and they were life. As he went up and down through Galilee, Judea and Peræa he was speaking the truth, proclaiming a new Gospel of God. He was bringing hope to a people who were all but hopeless, imparting faith to a people who were struggling with doubt and despair. He was bringing abundant life to a multitude who spiritually were lifeless. But these are general statements. The magic charm and power of Jesus' speech were due to some very definite affirmations.

How luminously Jesus spoke of God! Who else, either before Him or since has spoken of the heavenly Father in so intimate and revealing a way? He spoke of God as naturally and simply as a child speaks of father or mother. To Jesus God was not some awful Being far removed and remote, dwelling in unapproachable and awful majesty. He spoke of God as a heavenly Father who cares for His children, loves them, wills that joy be theirs. He chided the people for their unfaith, rebuked them for their slowness to believe. He called attention to God's care for the birds and the flowers and the grass, and said: "If God doth so clothe the grass of the field, which is today, and tomorrow is cast into the oven, shall He not much more clothe you, oh, ye of little faith?" Such words were as water to a thirsty throat.

Jesus was so sure of God. His consciousness of God, the divine nearness, infinite wisdom, unfathomable love, his sense of these was strong, abiding, satisfying. Our consciousness of God is fragmentary, broken, incomplete, partial. Sometimes He seems near; then again far, far removed from us. Sometimes we cannot sense Him at all, and there sweeps over us the cold wet winds of doubt and scepticism. But how different with Jesus! In all his contact with men and women and children he carried with Him, save for a brief terrible moment on the cross, this reassuring spirit or attitude of life. He recognized always the presence of the heavenly Father with whom he intimately conversed. "Have faith in God" was one of his quieting and inspiring counsels to his disciples in an experience that tried them sorely. He taught his disciples to pray to God, saying, "Our Father who art in heaven." He showed them the supremacy of love and service. He taught them that a man's life consisteth not in the abundance of the things he possesseth. To him God was greater than disaster, stronger than death. Surely no man ever spoke comparably to Jesus of Nazareth.

Joseph Fort Newton is of the opinion that "only God is permanently interesting"; and the most eminent theologians of our day aver the fundamental religious question to be one's idea of God. Mr. Ingersoll's famous twist of Alexander Pope's oft-quoted verse, "An honest God's the noblest work of man," is not as irreverent as the eloquent agnostic's critics claimed. It was an honest God that Jesus knew and loved and right honestly he proclaimed his heavenly Father to the world. Perhaps the highest view that Jesus set forth and the one we have been slowest to accept is his declaration to the woman at the well of Sychar that "God is a spirit and they who worship Him must worship Him in spirit and in truth." God as spirit is a theme for the devout theologian to muse upon and write about, an idea for the humblest believer to ponder on as he goes about his daily tasks. Verily, Jesus spoke luminously about God and shed a warm and mellow light in regions where shadows had hitherto reigned. Never man so spake of God as Jesus spoke.

How revealingly Jesus spoke of man. What an enigma man is! Consider his dreams, longings, aspirations, cruelties, tragedies; his iniquities, victories, defeats. Jesus knew what was in man. He knew the possibilities in man for good, courage, truth, and purity. And he also knew full well the possibilities in man for evil, falsehood, impurity, and cowardice. He knew all this, and despite this knowledge of the depths of degradation to which man can fall, he put a new and higher value on man; he made a new appraisal of man's worth in the eyes of God. He instanced the shepherd's concern for a single lost sheep from the flock, and he asked most searchingly the question, "How much more is a man worth than a sheep?" The implications of this query are staggering. When Jesus came man had no value save as his race, position, or possessions gave him; intrinsically humanity was as dumb driven cattle. Only a few counted when Jesus came. The rich counted; the nobility counted; the learned counted; but the poor, the outcast, the Publican—these counted not at all. Jesus taught that quite apart from his lot, his sin, his degradation, his rank, man counts; that God loves him and that all men are members of one family with a common Father. No truthful person pretends that this radical idea of brotherhood has found acceptance among Christians, but nevertheless it is of Jesus.

Jesus placed a new value on women and children. His disciples were surprised when they found him talking with a Samaritan woman whose reputation was not of the best. She herself was surprised, and marveled at his speech with her. If she was a "woman with a past" as seems likely, that speech she had with Jesus transformed her into a woman with a future—a new creature indeed. And where in any literature is there a story comparable with that of Jesus and the woman taken in adultery. His conduct under the circumstances, the extreme delicacy of feeling he indicated, and his tender, understanding speech with the accused who had flung herself at his feet, marked a new epoch for womankind. The slogan of the sea, "Women and children first," must have received its inspiration from Jesus of Nazareth, the friend of all women and the little children of the poor.

Jesus lifted the child to a new phase of importance in the community. Children flocked about him during his ministry. It is not recorded that this lover of humanity ever laughed or even smiled, but we may be sure that he did both, and for evidence there is the fact that the little children thronged about him and loved to be near him. Jesus put a child in the midst of his quarrelling disciples, a child that was near at hand, and said, "Except ye turn and become as little children ye shall in no wise enter into the Kingdom of Heaven: whosoever therefore shall humble himself as this little child the same is the greatest in the Kingdom of Heaven." Then there was that never-to-be-forgotten day in his ministry when the mothers brought their children to him that he might lay his hands upon them as a token of favor and affection. That was the day that his disciples believed him too busy to be disturbed by the little boys and girls of the neighborhood. They were mistaken, and Jesus rebuked them severely, saying, "Suffer the little children to come unto me and forbid them not, for of such is the Kingdom of Heaven.

"An' He that has ta'en us for kith and kin,
   Tho a Prince o' the far awa',
   Gaithert them roon Him whaur He sat,
   An' blisset them ane an' a'."

Is it any wonder that the common people heard Jesus gladly or that the officers sent to arrest him were arrested by his speech and returned without their prisoner, saying, "Never man so spake"?

How impressively Jesus spoke of life here and beyond the grave! Neither death nor life has been the same since he came. He did not attempt to prove immortality. He assumed that personality persists beyond the grave. Never man so spake of the unseen life. Who but he could say, "I am the resurrection and the life," and leave the impression on his hearers that he knew what he was talking about? He said, "Because I live ye shall live also"; and those who heard felt it must be true because Jesus said it. He did not talk about "jasper walls," "gates of pearl," or "street of gold"; rather he chose to speak of "my Father's house." He said that house was a roomy place, and to the millions who live in stuffy apartments and crowded tenement houses that idea of roominess is not without its appeal. To the dying penitent who hung upon the cross at his side, who pathetically asked, "Lord, remember me when thou comest into thy kingdom," He replied, "Today shalt thou be with me in Paradise." Nobody knows where Paradise is, or cares, for that matter, but the thought of companionship with Christ, here and hereafter, is replete with consolation and endless charm.

And of all that Jesus said of the ampler life that now is and yet to be, is anything quite so significant as his words, "I am the door"? What a curious and arresting figure of speech—Jesus, the door! Now what does a door signify?

Very much. One can judge the interior of a house by its door. Is the door shabby, paint peeling off, hanging on a single hinge? Then it opens into a house of the same character—run down, in disorder, unkempt. If, on the other hand the door be spacious, costly, ornamental, distinctive, one has a right to expect that the building into which it leads is splendid, spacious, beautiful. Surely this figure of Jesus as the door is enchanting! If Jesus is the door to life eternal, what must that life be? It cannot be less than Jesus. It must be as much as Jesus was to his disciples— that much and more! If he spake as never man spake of God and man and the hereafter, if he is the door to the larger life, then we need only to walk by faith in the comradeship of his unseen presence until the day break and the great door opens.

It must be apparent to the thoughtful and discerning that beyond and above anything that Jesus said about the life abundant his personality spoke more eloquently and convincingly still. Jesus' speech and deed synchronized perfectly. What he said he was. Those weighty words upon his lips concerning life, death, resurrection, seem consistent, logical, satisfying. Simon Peter, speaking on the day of Pentecost, averred that death was not able to hold Jesus. This is an appropriate affirmation. It fits the unique situation. What could death do permanently to so radiant a soul? How feeble and futile even "the last great enemy" appears in the presence of one who lived so intimately with God, whose thoughts and acts coincided so perfectly.

Never man so spake. The bewildered officials sent to arrest him, brought in the only verdict possible. He spake uniquely, he spake divinely. Jesus Christ is God's speech to the world, His epic poem, His autobiography. "In the beginning was the Word and the Word was with God, and

36

the Word was God." The author of the Hebrew epistle has a phrase that may well stand at the end of this sermon:

"God, having of old times spoken unto the fathers in the prophets, by diverse portions and in diverse manners, hath at the end of these days spoken unto us in His Son."

"Hear ye Him!"

JESUS—an UNFINISHED PORTRAIT

The old inquiry of the guests who had come up to Jerusalem for the festival, "Sir, we would see Jesus," is still being asked. The existing portraits of Jesus are many. Art, literature, theology, ritualism, institutionalism have done their best, but the likeness is dim. Only the portrait of Jesus as exhibited in character is satisfying and, alas, it too is unfinished.

IV

It was the last week of Jesus' life. The festival occasion was on and pilgrims filled Jerusalem to overflowing. Thus, into the center of worshipers, gathered from all points of the compass, came Jesus to his cross. There was a great deal of curiosity to see the Galilean prophet. Strange rumors were on the lips of the people. It was said that at Bethany, Jesus had brought back from the dead, Lazarus, the brother of Mary and Martha. Many tongues wagged and the excitement grew. Wherever Jesus and His disciples appeared on the streets of the city, crowds followed them. Certain Greeks who had come a long distance appealed to Philip, saying, "Sir, we would see Jesus." Moffatt translates it, "Sir, we want to see Jesus"; Weymouth, "Sir, we wish to see Jesus."

This request of the Greeks was perfectly natural. They had heard much about the new teacher. A reverent curiosity prompted their request to see him and possibly ask him a question. They were seekers after God, and while the record does not say so, I think we may infer that the Greeks saw Jesus, that they heard him speak and conversed with him about the deep things of the spirit.

For nineteen hundred years, multitudes have repeated the inquiry of the Greeks, "Sir, we would see Jesus." Moreover, a sincere attempt has been made to present Jesus not only to those who have expressed a desire to see Him, but also a passionate purpose to take a portrait of him into distant and hostile regions. The non-Christians, too, must see Jesus, for the missionary passion is born of him. Even among those who have grown up in a Christian environment and made familiar all their lives with the Christ of the churches, there has remained something of this wistful desire to experience a fuller vision, a deeper insight, a more adequate understanding of Jesus Christ.

Of portraits of Jesus, there have been many. Art has portrayed Jesus on imperishable canvases. Many of the famous masterpieces are scenes from his life—"Jesus in The Temple"; "Jesus and the Little Children"; "Jesus among His Disciples"; "Jesus on the Mount of Transfiguration"; "Jesus in the Garden"; "Jesus before Pilate"; "Jesus on the Cross." With such subjects the great painters have glorified their work. Christ in art is an interesting study, often inspiring, sometimes touching, nearly always impressive. But there are limitations. The Christ of the painters as works of art is one thing; as interpreters of the Jesus of Galilee, the portraits leave much to be desired.

There is no authentic painting of the Galilean prophet. Nobody knows how Jesus looked. There is no genuine description from which the artists might work. Imagination has achieved much in the field of religious art, yet it is always an unfinished portrait of Jesus that hangs on the walls of the famous galleries. "We would see Jesus" is the cry on the lips of those whose eyes are weary from gazing upon the Jesus of art. Masterpieces, indeed, but what would one not give for a glimpse of the Jesus that talked with the woman at Jacob's well!

Literature has contributed richly to the portrait of Jesus. There is a library of immense proportion on the subject. If all the volumes with Christ as theme could be assembled they would form a mountain of surprising size.

Nor could one estimate fairly the research, scholarship, intellectual acumen, patient investigation, prodigious labors represented in that literary mountain. There are the biographies, commentaries, encyclopedias, philosophic studies, poetry, drama, essays, and criticisms; the stream is full to the banks and seems endlessly flowing.

There are the famous Lives of Christ, by Geikie, Edershiem, Farrar, Strauss, Renan, Andrews, Nicoll, Hanna, Fleetwood, to list but a few. Some years ago a distinguished scholar, specializing in the realm of church history, declared it unlikely that other important Lives of Christ would be written; yet within the past decade have emerged notable biographies of Jesus by such famous authors as Papini, Rabbi Klausner, Ludwig, Case, Prof. Gilbert Murray, not to mention the hundreds of lesser known volumes having for subject the Founder of the Christian faith. The world's debt to the literary portrait of Jesus is very great, but it is an unfinished picture, and even the scholar, grown gray over much study, cries, "Sir, we would see Jesus."

Theology offers a notable portrait of Jesus. It is easy to belittle theology. There is a cheap way of disposing of theology with a languid wave of the hand, a sneer, a frown. Theology is not as important as religion, but it is important. Theology is preceded by religion as botany by plant life, or as geology by the structure of the earth. "Religion is the reality of which theology is the study." Theology is the science of religion, the opinions of man about God analyzed and systematized. There is no more reason for speaking contemptuously of theology than speaking in like manner of any science where the patient labor of the specialist is deserving of praise.

The trouble with theology is that it tends to become

fixed and dogmatic. The theologians and the creed-makers have only too often composed their portrait of Jesus and sought to give it an official imprimatur, saying, "This is the genuine portrait; all others are spurious." It is somewhat confusing, when you have a dozen portraits of Jesus by master theologians, each one saying, "This is the only genuine picture." It is an indisputable fact that most religious reformers have been suspicious and fearful of dogmatic theology. Some of these sturdy radicals, in their attempt to restore the New Testament portrait of Jesus, attacked theology vigorously and repudiated as tests of faith the doctrine of total hereditary depravity, the Adamic sin, imputed righteousness, eternal decrees, predestination and foreordination. They did not deny that there were elements of truth in the theological picture, they admitted as much, but they saw likewise distortion, error, and mischief, and boldly told the world what they saw.

There will always be a place for the theologian. The best minds in every generation should be at work upon the science of religion, musing about God, reflecting upon man, poring over history and studying the streams of thought of the times. A restatement of the great Christian doctrines in the light of present-day learning and modern conditions is needed in every generation, yet at its best, the theologian's portrait of Jesus is incomplete and men cry as they yearn for something not yet realized, "Sir, we would see Jesus."

Ritual has achieved a rich and rewarding portrait of Jesus. Religious pageantry is very old. The ancient Jewish faith stressed form and ceremony. Employing eloquent symbols and elaborate rites, the Jewish people worshiped God, making much of holy days, ceremonies, and festivals. The description in the Old Testament of the Jew at worship is aflame with color; the golden candlesticks, the Ark of the Covenant, the altar with its bleeding sacrifice, the singing of the vested choirs, the melodious temple music—all of this was an endeavor to interpret God, appealing to the eye and the ear. Christianity has made much of its symbols. One branch of the church has brought over something of the glorious ritual of Israel and given it a Christian setting—the pageantry of the Mass, the dramatization of the Crucifixion. What vivid coloring in this portrait of Jesus, and how strong the appeal to the deeply emotional!

Protestantism in its revolt from the ornate ritualism of the Catholic Church, swung far out to the opposite extreme, either to an austere simplicity or a breezy informality, lacking dignity, and suffered thereby. Now the tide is coming back and there is a distinct enrichment of worship in those churches known as nonliturgical and with a reputation for simplicity and democracy. The trend is unmistakable.

The symbols of Christianity belong to all the church, not part of it. No communion has a monopoly on the cross, the world-wide symbol of Christianity. The time has come when it is no longer possible to identify the particular body of Christians by the cross topping a tower or spire. An orderly service, processionals and recessionals, robed choirs, and even gowned ministers have replaced the haphazard, slipshod ways of conducting worship in some churches where a decade ago such an innovation would have divided congregations. This is significant. There can be no doubt of the appeal of a worshipful background and a reverent atmosphere to the soul of man. Dr. Theodore Munger, following a description of the services of the Anglican Church, adds the significant comment, "Here lies the secret of public worship; we do not worship because we feel like it, but that we may feel."

The appeal of religion is fourfold—to the eye, the ear, the mind, and the emotions. Ritualism, therefore, has its justification. Ritualism has painted the most vivid of all the portraits of Jesus, yet amid the stately ceremonies, the age-old symbols, gorgeous pageantry, the heart of many a worshiper has ached, and from quivering lips has come the prayer, "Sir, we would see Jesus." Ritual's portrait of our Lord, rich and elaborate, ornate and realistic, is unfinished, inadequate.

Institutionalism has contrived to present a portrait of the Christ all its own—the picture of a busy, bustling, efficient Master. There is something distinctly modern and of the Western World in this portrait. It shows Jesus as an organizer, a man of affairs, capable, industrious. The Institutional side of Christianity is a formidable affair. There are the vested interests, vast and sometimes sinister because of their vastness. Imposing arrays of statistics, tabulated to date and on exhibition. What a multiplicity of commissions, committees, societies, are enlisted and recorded in the name of Jesus. In some sections of the church there is a genius for organization and the thing is achieved after the most approved methods of office management. The phrase "selling religion" and even "selling Jesus" falls easily from the tongues of ecclesiastical promoters and occasionally appears in the religious press. There is, to be sure, a business side to the conduct of a church and the various societies formed for the promotion of by-products of Christianity, but these "side issues," when promoted aggressively and exploited out of all proportion, become deadly foes of the devotional life and spiritually-mindedness.

There are those who go so far as to hold that institutionalism has no place in Christianity, or, if so, a distinctly minor place. Discerning minds know only too well what over-organization will do to a local church—committees, societies, dinners, drives, innumerable activities, paraphernalia of the market place, the bazaar, and the carnival. It is not surprising that occasionally ministers leave the pastorate, giving the reason of one city pastor who resigned the pulpit, "in order to do religious work." A certain amount of organization is necessary in the propagation of the Christian faith, but the thing has been overdone and the reaction has left us cold. The point is that the picture of Jesus offered by institutionalism and organized Christianity is partial, inadequate, and disappointing. Great buildings, vast memberships, multifarious organization—these are imposing, often spectacular. Yet many a weary church worker has sighed amid the confusion of feverish activity and murmured, "Sir, we want to see Jesus."

The most satisfactory portrait of Jesus yet offered to the world is His spirit transforming human character. Your portrait of Christ may be more perfect than a del Sarto or a Raphael. Writing to one of the early churches, Paul said of them that they were "living letters, known and read of all men." This is high praise. The living portraits of Jesus have answered as nothing else the pathetic cry, "We would see Jesus." It is good to remember that Paul himself said that Christ lived in him, and in his writings he spoke of "Christ in you, the hope of glory."

It was this living portrait of Jesus in the hearts of those

47

early disciples that made them irresistible. When Stephen died outside the city wall with a prayer on his lips for those who stoned him, a young rabbi standing near him saw Jesus in Stephen's dying act and heard Jesus in Stephen's dying words. Stephen's portrait of Jesus started Saul on the way to Christ. When John and Peter were before the Jewish tribunal and forbidden, under pain of punishment, to preach or teach any more in the name of Jesus, they were startled by the answer of the two defenseless men, "Whether it be right in the sight of God for us to harken unto you rather than unto God, judge ye, for we cannot but speak the things which we have seen and heard." They saw Jesus in the lives of those two men transfigured by his spirit, all aflame with his passion for a redeemed humanity.

The romance and victory of the missionary enterprise is the story of living portraits of Jesus Christ. Mrs. Judson's lovely portrait of her Master broke down every barrier and enabled her to receive undreamed-of concessions from the Burma king which furthered the missionary cause. Recall Livingstone in Africa. What a portrait of Jesus! Stanley, the explorer, confessed that he was an atheist until he met Livingstone. What made Stanley a believer? The portrait of Jesus he saw in the life of David Livingstone. Just now the loveliest portrait of Jesus in India is mirrored in the life of E. Stanley Jones. But time would fail me if I spoke of John Wesley, who awakened a sleeping nation and a cold and indifferent church; of St. Francis of Assisi, so gentle of heart he called every living thing his brother; of John Bunyan, who went to jail for Jesus' sake; John Eliot brought to the American Indians a vision of One who possessed the Great Spirit; of General William Booth, who went out into the east end of London, saw the misery and the crime, and said, "I hunger for hell" and plunged into that hell only to bring there a bit of heaven; of Dr. Albert L. Shelton, who in far away Tibet brought to those who sat in darkness a shining light and a healing ministry; of a great host at home and abroad, in high places and in obscure corners of the earth, rich and poor, learned and ignorant, white and black and brown, men and women and little children in whose lives others saw Jesus and were glad.

The portrait of Jesus as exhibited in the character of those who have been captured by his spirit is the only Jesus that multitudes will ever see. Theology is a closed book to millions; elaborate rituals have slight appeal to host upon host who "the straight, hard path have trod"; organizations, however high-powered, leave myriads cold. But Jesus-like men and women, human beings who reflect the mind of Christ and possess his spirit, these in all verity are the light of the world and the salt of the earth. Yet even this portrait of Jesus, yours and mine—everybody's portrait of Jesus is unfinished.

> "Our little systems have their day;
> They have their day and cease to be;
> They are but broken lights of Thee,
> And Thou, O Lord, art more than they."

IS LIFE ANTI-CLIMAX?

So far as the physical eye can see, life appears to be a hard climb up a high hill, to stand for a brief period on the sunlit summit and then the long slow descent on the other side. By all material tokens we fade as a leaf. But is life really anti-climax? Just when are the so-called "palmy days"?

V

"We all do fade as a leaf."—Isaiah LXIV:6
"For we know that if the earthly house of our bodily frame be dissolved, we have a building from God, a house not made with hands, eternal in the heavens."

II Cor. V:1

Is life anti-climax? Are the days of youth golden, the years of middle life mellow, rich, and old age lame and lusterless? Is one half of life a hard struggle up a high hill, to stand for a brief period on the sunlit summit, and the other half a going down the hill on the other side, to disappear in darkness and gloom? Is the life we live destined to be anti-climax?

On the surface it appears to be. The somber, mournful music of Robert G. Ingersoll's words at the graveside of his brother have in them the semblance of truth. What beautiful words, and yet how pensive they are:

"Whether in mid-sea or 'mong the breakers of the farther shore, a wreck at last must mark the end of each and all. And every life, no matter if its every hour is rich with love and every moment jeweled with a joy, will, at its close, become a tragedy as sad and deep and dark as can be woven of the warp and woof of mystery and death."

So far as the natural man can perceive, these words of the famed agnostic, alas, are true. Moreover, the thought might be carried farther and pressed to a conclusion even apart from death, which is the theme of the orator, the "tragedy"

53

to which he referred. So far as the physical eye can see, life appears to be anti-climax.

Look at man's physical life. "We all do fade as a leaf." This is a melancholy statement. It is not pleasant to contemplate, but this fading of bodily powers is true. Physical humanity has its seasons even as nature, spring and summer, autumn and winter. The passing years take their toll from the body. The eye dims, the hearing becomes less acute, the hair silvers, the muscles grow inelastic. One tires more easily, the body becomes a prey to the invasion of disease. "We all do fade as a leaf." And some day the leaf will fall from the tree. Apparently, physical life is anti-climax.

The intellectual life, on the whole, is less affected by this fading process and there are many whose minds have steadily developed and almost to the end of advanced age have preserved brilliance and beauty. But usually these are exceptional persons who by inheritance or discipline have achieved this distinction. As a rule, the close relationship between body and mind means that as bodily vigor fades the mind is in one way or other affected thereby. The ability to concentrate is involved; memory plays unwonted pranks. Taking the broad view of mankind, there are good reasons for concluding that the intellectual life is anti-climax.

Consider the matter of creature comforts, freedom from domestic worry and financial anxieties. Men and women who have worked hard and met courageously life's vicissitudes deserve in old age a comfortable home, encircled with love, fragrant with sympathy. But how often it is otherwise. Most of us can recall pathetic instances in the lives of friends and kinspeople whose latter days have been less comfortable, storm swept, and more exacting than in other years. If life is to be assessed according to material rewards, then it is often anti-climax.

In the realm of human greatness, genius and fame, the close of life to men whose names were on a million tongues in acclamation is often harsh and unheroic. To those who have died amid crises and at the very zenith of their fame, fortune has seemed kind—Lovejoy, Lincoln, Garfield, McKinley. Napoleon finished his amazing career an exile, his days of flame and color over, at the age of fifty-one on St. Helena. A hundred years ago in this country three shining figures filled the political canvas; Henry Clay, Daniel Webster, and John C. Calhoun were the political darlings at that time. Their heyday of glory was not at the end, but in the later middle of their careers. They yearned for the grand prize of the Presidency and died bitterly disappointed. Take the case of Theodore Roosevelt, who came to the Presidency at the age of forty-three. What a mighty hour was his upon the stage of American political life! What a picturesque actor, and how he captured our imagination! Yet in a way the closing days of his life were anti-climax. We have his own confession that after a man has been President of the United States nothing else quite satisfies him. Even the biggest task seems trivial as compared with that exalted office. His last years were filled with political controversy, and while he still numbered his friends by the millions, the glamour and the fame belonged mostly to the past. Think of Woodrow Wilson, who for three-fourths of his life enjoyed academic and literary delights. Recall his years of philosophic calm; the days spent in the charm of academic circles; his sudden rise to world fame, and for a little while splendidly enthroned upon the dizzy heights of earthly glory such as comes to only few human beings; then as suddenly engulfed in detraction and defeat, broken in body, broken politically, broken every way except spiritually. From the human viewpoint Wilson's life was anti-climax, terribly so; whether it was really so or not is an intriguing question that time will answer.

There also is the case of William Jennings Bryan, who for thirty years or more was a persuasive and engaging leader, eloquent of tongue, who spoke to more people face to face than any other American, and was three times a candidate for the Presidency. It would seem that an arc would describe Mr. Bryan's career, a curved line rising rapidly to its zenith, say in 1912, and then dropping to what happened at Dayton, Tennessee, in 1925. Perhaps nine people out of ten, if asked the question, "Was Bryan's life anti-climax?" would say, "It was!" But was it? The verdict of history is not yet in, but, judging the present by the past, no one can say of a surety whether or not a contemporary has failed or succeeded. There is so much of victory in defeat and so much of defeat in victory that it does not become any of us to be unduly elated over success or cast down by failure.

"We all do fade as a leaf," and the day comes when the leaf falls from the tree—falls in storm or gently from the old forsaken bough.

"The silver chord is loosed, the golden bowl is broken, the pitcher is broken at the fountain, the wheel broken at the cistern, and the dust returneth to the earth as it was, and the spirit returneth unto God who gave it."

This is the "wreck" that Ingersoll had in mind. This is the "tragedy" on which he mused so mournfully. Death, the destroyer; but as Browning says, in "Paracelsus":

BLUNDERING INTO PARADISE

"If I stoop
Into a dark tremendous sea of cloud,
It is but for a time; I press God's lamp
Close to my breast; its splendor, soon or late,
Will pierce the gloom; I shall emerge one day."

We shall have to concede that life as the physical eye perceives it is anti-climax. But the view is partial; the argument incomplete. Only one side of the shield is shown. To take a surface view of life and straightway conclude that the end is disaster and defeat is like a man who has lived all his life in the tropics and beholds for the first time a northern landscape in winter, and looking about him at the dreary stretch of leafless trees and snow-blanketed earth, exclaims, "Alas! this woodland will never again be crowned with verdure and the beauty of spring has departed for all time." Or again, such logic is like a man watching the scarlet sunset of a perfect day, and as twilight deepens and darkness comes on cries: "This day is done forever. There will never again be such a day. Night is the enemy of day." The analogy, of course, is imperfect; but it is suggestive. Furthermore, to bemoan the passing of spring because winter is here, and the dying of the day because night enshrouds the earth in darkness, is to refuse to see the mission of winter, snow and ice and their part in the economy of nature; is to ignore the ministry of darkness and the rest that comes in sleep; and to take a one-sided, irrational view of life. Nature is never anti-climax, no matter what happens. Nor is human life anti-climax, save where the individual wills that it shall be so or society is recreant in its community burden-bearing and neighborly concern. Even so the returns are not all in.

Is life anti-climax? Turn to the Bible, that age-old literature which is neither primarily scientific nor a cross-word

57

puzzle of prophecy, but a book of religion, depicting humanity in its relation to God, the religious aspirations of a remarkable race, and the historic beginnings of the Christian order. Take the Old Testament. Turn to the Ninetieth Psalm, one of the most majestic of all the Psalms. The first half of this Psalm seems to view life as anti-climactic, the picture is somber in the extreme. "We spend our years as a tale that is told," wails the writer, and continues:

> "The days of our years are threescore years and ten,
> Or even by reason of strength fourscore years;
> Yet is their pride but labor and sorrow;
> For it is soon gone, and we fly away."

This is dirge-like music. But suddenly another and a different note is struck:

> "So teach us to number our days,
> That we may get us a heart of wisdom . . .
> Oh satisfy us in the morning with thy lovingkindness,
> That we may rejoice and be glad all our days."

This is better, nobler; and now comes the mighty conclusion:

> "Let thy work appear unto thy servants,
> And thy glory upon thy children.
> And let the beauty of the Lord our God be upon us;
> And establish thou the work of our hands upon us;
> Yea, the work of our hands establish thou it."

Yes, the "beauty" of the Lord—that makes all the difference in the world. And the establishing of the work of our hands by Almighty God—what a beneficent boon— the very idea is inspiring. This Ninetieth Psalm is commended as a prescription for those who take the view that

58

"Every life, no matter if its every hour be rich with love and every moment jeweled with joy will, at its close, become a tragedy as sad and deep and dark as can be woven of the warp and woof of mystery and death."

There is healing and help in this Psalm of life.

Survey the New Testament, the Christian Bible. How fares this question there? Is life viewed in its pages as anticlimax? The answer is a thunderous "No!" There is an embarrassment of riches, but take II Corinthians, one of the most thoughtful sections of the writings of St. Paul. Listen!

"But we have this treasure in earthen vessels. . . . We are pressed on every side, yet not straitened; perplexed, yet not unto despair; pursued, yet not forsaken; smitten down, yet not destroyed."

That describes every human life at some period, and some lives the greater part of the time. But harken.

"Wherefore we faint not; but though our outward man is decaying, yet our inward man is renewed day by day. . . . While we look not at the things which are seen, but at the things which are not seen; for the things which are seen are temporal; but the things which are not seen are eternal."

Now this is lofty teaching. Here is an affirmation of the reality of the unseen. Therefore, you cannot measure life, appraise or interpret life, by what is seen upon the surface of things. You must dig deeper, climb higher, survey the whole of life; then, and not until then, make your conclusions.

Life is more than food and clothing; life is more than shelter and possessions. Man cannot live by bread alone. Poverty is inconvenient, burdensome, yet nevertheless from the ranks of the poor and disinherited have come the world's leaders and liberators, almost without exception; the great geniuses, the names that were not born to die. Health has a great deal to do with happiness; sickness is a handicap, but Robert Louis Stevenson was greater than the consumption that cut him off a little beyond middle life. John Keats, battling with the same disease, wrote his immortal poems and died in his prime. Alexander Pope was a cripple, but life with him was climactic. There is something in the spirit of man greater than the physical man, stronger even than the intellectual man. Who is the most potent spiritual personality in the world today? Undoubtedly Mahatma Gandhi, the seer of India, who weighs less than a hundred pounds, a little, emaciated figure and not prepossessing; stripped of all his earthly possessions, imprisoned, yet powerful for good. Great ideas are immortal; sublime sacrifices are deathless. Man, plus the Spirit of God, is destined to overcome even death, the last great enemy.

Jesus died at the age of thirty-three, a young man. His public life consisted of three crowded years. The first year of this public ministry saw him reach the height of his popularity. Great crowds hung upon his every utterance. The common people heard him gladly. The multitudes thronged him; they wished to make him king. Then he began to announce his death, spoke of the cross upon which he must die. His disciples held back. He became engulfed in controversy. His enemies conspired to put him to death. One of his own intimate friends betrayed him. At his makeshift of a trial justice was missing. They hurried him to the cross, where, amid the taunts of the rabble, he died the death of a criminal. Everything seemed over. His bright dream ended. His followers, now scattered, were like poor, foolish, frightened sheep without a shepherd. Judged by all external things, the death of Jesus of Nazareth was cruelly, terribly anti-climax. Aye, but actually, his death on the cross crowned his life forever; made him the Saviour of the world and our divinest symbol. Through death he won the grandest of victories—"Crown him with many crowns."

I recall once hearing an enthusiastic student of the life and times of St. Paul say that from the short view the Apostle made shipwreck of his life. Then he instanced the bitter disappointment of his family when the young scholar espoused the cause of the infant church, the dire disillusionment of his fellow Jews when he turned his back on a rabbinical career of alluring brilliance, the high cost of renunciation of his family, childhood faith, secure position, ease and comfort, his sufferings by land and sea, and at last death by violence. Shipwreck, indeed, was the life of Paul as appraised by those who were on "the other side." But history has another view, time a different estimate, eternity a rosier judgment.

I cannot refrain from quoting here a glorious paragraph from a sermon preached nearly half a century ago by Leonard Woolsey Bacon on "The Petition of Certain Greeks." Listen to the organ music of his splendid words: "The history of the advancement of Christ's Kingdom is a long record of sore disappointments. You may go to the old burying-ground of Northampton, Massachusetts, and look upon the early grave of David Brainard, side by side with that of the fair Jerusha Edwards, whom he loved but did not live to wed. What hopes, what expectations for Christ's cause went down into the grave with the wasted form of that young missionary of whose work nothing now remains but the dear memory and a few score of swarthy

Indian converts! But that majestic old Puritan saint, Jonathan Edwards, who had hoped to call him son, gathered up the memorials of his life in a little book. And the book took wings and flew beyond the sea, and alighted on the table of a Cambridge student—Henry Martyn. Poor Martyn! Why would he throw himself away with all his scholarship, his genius—his opportunities! Such a wasted life it seemed! What had he accomplished when he turned homeward from "India's coral strand," broken in health, and dragged himself northward as far as that dreary kahn at Tocat by the Black Sea, where he crouched under the piled-up saddles, to cool his burning fever against the earth, and there died alone, among unbelievers, no Christian hand to tend his agony, no Christian voice to speak in his ear the promises of the Master, whom, as it seemed to man, he had so vainly served. To what purpose was this waste?"

"We know that if the earthly house of this bodily frame be dissolved we have a building from God, a house not made with hands, eternal in the heavens." Again, St. Paul, "We know" that neither life nor death is anti-climax! I recall a modern commentary on this statement of the mightiest of the apostles—a story that floods the words with light. It has to do with John Quincy Adams of that famous House of Adams. This President of the United States, who was the son of another President, was the greatest of all the Adamses in the opinion of the author of *The Adams Family*. Highly educated, trained in diplomacy and politics, of unimpeachable personal integrity, he served his country in several important missions abroad, Secretary of State under Monroe; President for one term and afterward gave eighteen years of high service in the House of Representatives, where his vigorous mind and eloquent tongue championed the cause of the slave, to the defense of what he felt to be the highest standards of public and private conduct. In his old age some one met this great old man on the streets of Washington, bowed courteously, and inquired, "And how is John Quincy Adams this morning?" The venerable statesman replied, "Well, sir, the house in which John Quincy Adams lives is dilapidated, the roof, sir, is leaking, the walls are shaking, the foundation is trembling, but as for John Quincy Adams himself, he is very well, sir, never better, sir." Aye, this is the right view, the long view, the Christian view.

Robert Browning was a seer, and, some hold, the most Christian of our poets. In "Rabbi Ben Ezra" Browning answers this question—Is life anti-climax?

> "Grow old along with me!
> The best is yet to be,
> The last of life, for which the first was made;
> Our times are in His hands
> Who saith, A whole I planned,
> Youth shows but half; trust God;
> See all, nor be afraid."

Therefore, face life with head up. Think life, not death. Think love, not hate. Put the emphasis upon the affirmative. "Look up, not down," as good old Edward Everett Hale would say, "and lend a hand." It is not true that man is as old as his arteries—man is as old as his faith, his hope, his love; *the best is yet to be!*"

The DISCIPLINE of DELAYED REVELATION

Jesus could not reveal himself fully to his disciples, for the good reason that they were not prepared to receive the revelation. In truth, revelation awaits capacity and capacity depends upon time and experience. Nature gives up her secrets to the inquiring mind, one by one, not all at once, but through vast stretches of time. Time is a wise teacher, but no wiser than experience. "Live and learn" is a good life motto.

VI

"I have yet many things to say unto you but you cannot bear them now."

John XVI:12

The place is an upper room somewhere in Jerusalem; the time, the last night of Jesus before his crucifixion; the occasion, his meeting with his disciples to observe the passover, institute the memorial supper, and to talk with them never so intimately.

In this sixteenth chapter of St. John's gospel occurs the verse, "Ye did not choose me, but I chose you." The thought that Christ discovers us rather than that we discover him, that his is the love that will not let us go, is a doctrine on the one hand almost too good to be true, and on the other, one that lays upon the individual a deep and impressive obligation.

To range the present-day disciples of our Lord alongside those early followers of his, especially the Twelve, seems at first blush presumptuous. But is it? I will admit, of course, that his choice of the Twelve differed from his choice of us in degree, but not in essence. We are accustomed to dwell on the Godward side of things, to stress and emphasize what God is doing for us, what he means to us. Might it not be profitable to turn to the other side of the shield? The manward side is the uncertain side. This is why it is good for us to think seriously on what we mean to Jesus Christ.

There is something breath-taking in the idea that God

needs us, must have us. Nay, let me put it stronger—the thought that our Lord is depending upon us, that Christ cannot further his kingdom save through his disciples, that God himself is incomplete without his children, is overwhelming and revolutionary. But such is the spirit of the Gospel.

"I have yet many things to say unto you, but you cannot bear them now." Jesus had told his disciples as much as they were prepared to receive. He had answered their questions, quieted their fears, quickened their imaginations. He had given them something to think about, food for reflection, for the rest of their lives. But Jesus was not through. He had other things to tell his disciples, but might not tell them now. They were not ready to receive them. Their hearts were too full, their minds troubled, they were a little bewildered. For the time being, Jesus had taught them all that he could teach them; that is, all that they were able to bear. He reserved till a later time further teaching. He postponed additional enlightenment. He had taken them as far as they could go; but not so far as he hoped they would go.

Revelation awaits capacity and capacity depends on time and experience. How much can parents tell their children of life and the issues that belong to maturity? Very, very little. A hint here, a suggestion there, the unfolding of this, the disclosure of that, and these not all at once but gradually. The reason is obvious. Our children are not prepared to receive all that we have to say to them. Even the most splendid mind among the apostles of Christ confessed, "When I was a child, I spake as a child, I felt as a child; now that I am become a man I have put away childish

68

things." How far is it from childhood to maturity? Farther than most of us care to confess.

I remember once trying to talk to a little boy about death. His sister had died and he was mystified, perplexed, dazed. Why had she died and where had she gone? How little I could tell him that he was prepared to receive. But I tried and I am sure I comforted his heavy heart, not so much by what I said as by my attitude of trust. Yet all the while I, too, was wondering, questioning, seeking light, a baffled learner in the school of life. Thus does it go on endlessly, this quest for truth, and all the while humanity awaits the capacity to receive God.

The revelation of truth throughout the universe and in all ages is gradual and progressive. There are those who conceive of truth as a block of marble, so many feet wide, so many feet high. They say with zest: "Here it is. Here is truth. Take a look at it, measure it, but you mustn't break or chip it; it is complete, perfect. Be careful not to mar it." A better symbol of truth, and certainly a more accurate one, is a stream fed by springs, broadened and deepened by many tributaries, ever widening, mingling somewhere at last its waters with old ocean. It is good to be able to say, "Take a look at this stream; see it is never still; behold it is moving, deepening, widening." Truth is something like this. Yet even this figure of a stream is inadequate. Truth cannot be fully described by the finest of figures.

The revelation of God in the Bible is progressive, the idea of God there ever expanding. The conception of God as held by the ancient Jewish race was much finer and loftier than that held by other peoples; yet the Jewish conception of Jehovah is a growing one, beginning with the

69

idea of a tribal god, a territorial god, a national Deity. Here and there in Old Testament times a seer, poet, or prophet was capable of receiving a larger, richer, juster idea of God. Thus we have mountain peaks of revelation in the Old Testament lifting themselves far above their humbler fellows, as when Micah speaks, "He hath showed thee, O man, what is good; and what doth the Lord require of thee, but to do justly and to love kindness, and to walk humbly with thy God?" Possibly the most advanced revelation of God in the Old Testament is that set forth by the Book of Jonah, which is in reality a mighty missionary tract designed to teach the universality of God's love.

Even in the New Testament revelation of truth is progressive. Between Mark's memoirs of Jesus and John's interpretation is something more than the element of time. It would appear that thirteen of the epistles were written by Paul, that I Thessalonians was the earliest and Philippians of a much later date. The mind of Paul as revealed in these letters was expanding. He moved onward and upward. His interpretation becomes more spiritual. He finds himself at odds with the narrow nationalistic groups among the early Christians. He is a growing Christian to the end of his days. Professor James H. Snowden calls Paul the master modernist and in half a dozen pages traces the growth of this, the greatest of the apostles, who concluded before he finished his course that love is greater than hope, greater than faith, greater than knowledge, greater than martyrdom, far greater than charity, the greatest thing in all the world.

The divine teacher cannot himself impart knowledge until the capacity of the pupil is sufficient to receive that knowledge. And here too the time element enters into the matter. Days and weeks, months and years, must sometimes elapse before one learns how to live the life of the spirit. Nor is his education in this realm, as in any other, ever completed. "Cast thy bread upon the waters; for thou shalt find it after many days." How many days? Nobody knows, but *find* it "thou shalt"; that is the all-important matter.

God's revelation of Himself and His purposes are delayed of necessity. "The slow years," to use that fine phrase of James Russell Lowell, are a mighty factor. Processes of evolution are slow in nature. Talk of the "law's delays," what about the delays of nature? How old is this earth of ours? Archbishop Ussher was extremely cautious in his guess of six thousand years. Six million years may be conservative. Nobody knows of a certainty, but the truth is on the side of the antiquity of the earth. It takes a vast stretch of time, eons, indeed, to produce coal. Compared with the age of the rocks Christianity is a babe in swaddling clothes.

The processes of the Creator in nature are gradations through years, centuries, ages. Not only the rocks are stratified; so are nations and individuals.

> "A fire-mist, and a planet,—
> A crystal and a cell,--
> A jellyfish and a saurian
> And caves where cave men dwell;
> Then a sense of law and beauty,
> And a face turned from the clod.
> Some call it Evolution
> Others call it God."[1]

Time is a wise old teacher. We can never quite understand the things that try us, the temptations that assail us,

[1] William Herbert Carruth in "Each in His Own Tongue and Other Poems." G. P. Putnam's Sons, New York.

the ministry of suffering and pain, until Time, the great healer, has wrought his perfect work. One of the scholars of the church, none other than Principal Rainy, declared that there were times when God seems dumb. Dumb, indeed! We cry aloud and He does not answer. We listen and hear not the faintest whisper from the Almighty. We set our hearts upon a certain desired goal. It seems a reasonable, not a sordid, ambition. If God is like Christ, the achievement of that goal seems to be part of our Christian expectancy. But, lo! disappointment, bitter failure, cruel disaster, crowd upon us, and in our sense of failure and humiliation we begin to doubt not only the goodness of God, but His existence.

We build a home and gather there that holy institution, a family; affliction is visited upon a little child; death takes away a youth in all its splendid promise and beauty. Our homes are smitten at their four corners, and amid the darkness and the doubt we say with Jacob, in the hour of his suffering, "All things are against me," and so it seems. Time, and time alone, can answer the questions that assail us and will not down. Five, ten, twenty, maybe forty years before the answer comes. By that time our capacity for receiving the answer may be sufficiently developed and we get the answer fully, satisfying, ennobling. Or maybe the answer never comes in this life, but beyond! Another life is a necessity if God be just and this life justified.

What a boon it is that we do not know what tomorrow may bring!

"Life is so kind never to let us know
    The last time we go down the long, steep hill,
  Never to know when falls the last soft snow,
    Nor what bright bird will be the last to trill;

Never to know what joy will be the last,
  Nor when fleet youth will turn and wing away,
Nor to have presage that the height is past
  Of that brief passion which no love can stay.

Life is so kind—far kinder than we dream—
  When bitter pain and overwhelming grief
Darken the hours, nor give us then a gleam
  Of silver spray across death-blackened reef.
If I had known that day you were to die,
I never, never could have said good-bye."[1]

"I have yet many things to say unto you, but you cannot
bear them now." Experience is a strong and wise teacher.
What can we know about temptation until we have battled
with it? What do we know about pain and suffering until
we have grappled with the experience? What do we know
about disappointment until we have tasted it to the dregs?
What can we know about death until it comes close, invades
the homes of our friends, our own family circle? Even so,
how long the waiting before we catch the clue to the
enigma? What, pray, becomes of our trust in "a God who
cares," "special providences," the love that will not let us
go? Where is our God and why has He forsaken us?

The answer to these poignant questions can come only
when experience has done her perfect work. Every pastor
has observed the immediate effect of shock, disaster, and
loss upon the men and women of his congregation. Usually there is a period of rebellion, of terrible doubt, a with-
drawing from church activities and social relationships.
Some make the necessary adjustments sooner than others,
due perhaps to sanguine temperament and a legacy of
health and optimism. Others are a long time coming to

[1] Edith Lombard Squires in the *New York Times*.

themselves, are critical, censorious, bitter. It is a time for consideration on the part of friends, for a demonstration of understanding and tenderest sympathy. To all such cases we should bring that attitude of mind and heart such as we could wish might be shown us when all our best-laid plans go wrong and our house of hope tumbles to ruin.

"I have many things yet to say unto you, but you cannot bear them now." Every day brings new reasons for regarding these words of Jesus thoughtfully, perseveringly. Take that frightful disaster which occurred recently in the little Michigan town of Bath. A madman explodes a stick of dynamite, destroys a school building, blots out the lives of forty human beings, mostly children. The little town is shaken as by earthquake shock. Imagine yourself a father or mother in that town that awful day, the life of your little boy or girl crushed out—the work of a maniac. The thing might have happened to any of us. Such things are happening all around us every day. It will take years for that community to recover from the shock, and in some instances even time itself will be short to assuage wholly the grief. Yet do not doubt that from that community and the families of those where death wrought havoc in the long, long run of human affairs will emerge certain by-products on the side of goodness and gain. One by-product of this calamity at Bath has already appeared—I mean the timely and beneficent gift of Senator James Couzens of one hundred thousand dollars to that afflicted community This is something, but it is not all, nor is it the most lasting aftermath of an inexplicable tragedy.

I have been rereading *The Letters of Franklin K. Lane*. Here was one of our eminent fellow citizens, Woodrow Wilson's Secretary of the Interior, and a man of parts. Blest for the greater part of his life with perfect health, in love with the beauty of this world, of men and books, music and pictures, mountain and sea, the last months of Franklin K. Lane were filled with suffering and intimate acquaintance with operating-rooms and the surgeon's knife. In those days, facing the unknown, his mind intrigued by the mystery of existence, he whiled away the snail-paced hours by writing his mystic broodings as he pondered the sweet and awful mystery of life. Here follows the last paragraph of his last manuscript written the last day of his life:

"But for my heart's content in that new land, I think I'd rather loaf with Lincoln along a river bank. I know I could understand him. I would not have to learn who were his friends and who his enemies, what theories he was committed to, and what against. We could just talk and open out our minds, and tell our doubts and swap the longings of our hearts that others never heard of. He wouldn't try to master me nor to make me feel how small I was. I'd dare to ask him things and know that he felt awkward about them, too. And I would find, I know I would, that he had hit his shin just on those very stumps that had hit me. We'd talk of men a lot, the kind they call the great. I would not find him scornful. Yet boys that he knew in New Salem would somehow appear larger in their souls, than some of these that I had called the great. His wise eyes saw qualities that weighed more than smartness. Yes, we would sit down where the bank sloped gently to the quiet stream and glance at the picture of our people, the negroes being lynched, the miners' civil war, labor's hold-ups, employers' ruthlessness, the subordination of humanity to industry. . . ."

This is my idea of that "new land," too—the lifting of the horizons, renewals of old comradeships and glorious adventures in company with heroic souls who gave their all for the liberation of humankind. God has many things to tell us here and now and through the years. But I can well believe that some things will have to await His telling until the day break and all the shadows flee away. "I have yet many things to say unto you, but you cannot bear them now."

"Meantime the silent lip,
Meantime the climbing feet."

CHRISTIANITY and the ORDINARY MAN

The Christian movement began with a group of Galilean fishermen, artisans, and their women. These humble Palestinians, plus the spirit of God, shook the world. Today the drift of the masses is away from the churches. Why is this so and what can be done about it?

VII

In the sixteenth chapter of Romans, from a veritable catalogue of names this excerpt is taken:

"Greet Priscilla and Aquila, my helpers in Christ Jesus: who have for my life laid down their own necks: unto whom not only I give thanks but also all the churches of the Gentiles. . . . Greet Amplias, my beloved in the Lord. Salute Urbane, our helper in Christ. . . . Greet them that be of the house of Narcissus, which are in the Lord. . . . Salute Rufus, chosen in the Lord; and his mother and mine."

This curious and diverting chapter deserves to be read and studied. It is what a modern newspaper man would call "a human document." The social nature of the greatest of the apostles is revealed here and the chapter also indicates the spirit of hospitality that existed among the early Christians. There are thirty-five persons mentioned in this sixteenth chapter of Romans, and eight of them are women. Of the thirty-five, not more than half a dozen are familiar to a student of the Scriptures. This is the first time we come across these names, and the last. They appear only to disappear. They are representative of that huge majority which in any movement is obscure and unknown yet potent, loyal, influential, and without which no cause could triumph. In his correspondence with the Corinthians, St. Paul refers to those who composed the first-century church in an eloquent sentence, "Not many wise after the flesh, not many mighty, not many noble are called." It was ever so; the rank and file, the average human being—through and by them a movement conquers.

In the beginning of his ministry Jesus chose twelve men to be with him, learn of him and after his death proclaim his gospel to all nations. What manner of men did he chose and from what stations of society? Consider the twelve in pairs and what do we find?

Simon Peter, and Andrew his brother, were fishermen of Galilee. Peter was a man of parts, very human, impetuous, aggressive and at his best splendidly brave. Peter had the stuff of a pioneer in him. Andrew is famed for just one thing—he brought his more brilliant brother to Christ, and that was enough to give him a place in the sun.

James and John were sons of Zebedee, a Galilean fisherman. John was a rare soul, a good deal of a poet, and his writings about Jesus and the new way of life in him make humanity his debtor. No wonder "John" is the most popular name for a boy baby in the world. In French it is "Jean"; in Spanish, "Juan"; in German, "Johann"; in Russian, "Ivan"; in Dutch, "Jan"; in Italian "Giovanni." James, John's brother, is lost in the shadows. This is not the James who wrote the epistle by that name, who was a mighty man in the Jerusalem church. This James died early, a martyr for the cause. We might properly call him "James the Obscure."

Philip and Nathanael are vague figures. Philip had a habit of asking questions for which he deserves credit. Nathanael was guileless, a good man, but we do not know much about him—he fades out of the picture early in the story.

Thomas and Matthew occupy a higher niche. Thomas is interesting and not a little pathetic. His strain of scepticism is sincere and he gave evidence of devotion and loyalty. Matthew was a converted tax-gatherer, which implies he had business ability and courage. His memoir of his Master gives him a lofty place in Christian history.

James the son of Alpheus is in a way the most shadowy figure of the twelve. Nothing is known of him save that he was one of the Twelve. Jude was the half-brother of Jesus and brother of the James who wrote the epistle that bears his name. Jude's literary achievement is light in bulk, but the benediction with which his short letter closes entitles him to a niche in the hall of fame.

Simon the Zealot and Judas Iscariot were a strange pair. This Simon was a member of the revolutionary party of the Jews, an intense nationalist, but his figure is dim. As for this Judas, *the* Judas of Christian history, there is reason to believe he was the master mind of the Twelve, but for some reason not wholly clear he missed the mark and is numbered among the traitors.

Such were the twelve intimates of Jesus, the men whom he trusted to interpret his teaching to the world. Of the Twelve, eight are not much more than names, yet these were the key men of the Kingdom. Not one of the famous men of that day are included among the Twelve; no eminent merchant, orator, poet, or soldier is on the list. The Twelve are a cross section of the Palestinian country, the rank and file, the common people; and these men, plus the spirit of God, turned the world upside down.

So much for the disciples of Jesus, the Twelve, but what of the Master of them all? Let a vagrant verse bearing the title, "The Son of God," make answer:

> "He did not see Jerusalem—
> Nor Rome;
> He passed by all "best families"
> To dwell at last in Nazareth,

With Mary,
Mother of that Son
Who fraternized with fishermen;
Found heaven in little children;
And had a friend
Named Mary Magdalene."

The essence of Christian democracy is a sturdy belief in the average man and the duty to reckon with him always. Without the enlistment of the average citizen no battle can be won, no great cause furthered. Every political leader knows this and rightly or wrongly tries to capture the imagination of the rank and file, appeals to their prejudices, feeds their vanity, plays upon every human emotion in order to swing the masses to his party or candidacy. The doctrine that rightly informed the average man can be counted upon to respond to noble appeals and sacrificial labors, for human betterment is at least seventeen hundred years older than Thomas Jefferson.

Sometimes I have a suspicion that the typical church of our day quite unconsciously rates the average man meanly. This suspicion is confirmed when I read telegrams in certain religious weeklies reporting revivals of this character:

"Great services Sunday. Mayor of city and two bankers converted. Great rejoicing."

Now I freely admit that mayors and bankers need conversion, but for a change I for one would welcome a telegram to this effect:

"Great service in progress here. Two policemen, three garage men, two plumbers, five bookkeepers, and twenty children join church."

At any rate, a telegram of this nature would quicken the hope that Protestantism was getting back to the people and not losing its head in the presence of wealth and official-dom. The James who wrote the twentieth book of the New Testament observed a tendency to despise the common man and rebuked it in terms of great severity. "Ye have despised the poor. . . . Ye have respect to him that weareth the gay clothing. . . . If ye have respect of persons ye commit sin." Aye, it is not easy to love all people alike, nor am I sure it is possible; but I maintain the average man is a factor to be reckoned with, a power for good when his confidence is won and his loyalties enlisted. Further-more, the future of religion rests not with the exceptional man, the privileged and the scholar, but with the so-called common people.

What has the average man to bring to Christianity, organized Christianity, the church, if you please? His prejudices? To be sure, we all have them. His limitations? Granted—who is without them? But the average man brings something finer, better, nobler than his limitations and prejudices. He brings *fidelity*. If the history of the average man were written, the story of his everyday life in city, town, and country would abound in illustrations of his fidelity to his work, home, family, community. The life of the average man is jeweled with unheralded fidelities as he meets life, shoulders responsibilities, faces difficult tasks, lives through dark days. And there is a premium on fidelity. Faithfulness is a noble grace. It is possible and highly probable that the Christian religion has been propagated oftener and more powerfully by the fidelity of the average man and woman than by the genius and greater gifts of the exceptional adherent whose contribution was mostly intellectual or financial.

Some years ago, according to Bishop McDowell, there was a missionary, an Englishman, stationed in India who never could keep his accounts and finances in order. He was many times chided and rebuked by the Home Board, but always in vain. He simply could not keep his books straight. So the Home Board relieved him of his position and sent a man in his place who was a good bookkeeper. The missionary who was dismissed, instead of going home to England, went off on his own account in a new section of India where no missionary had ever gone before. Many years passed and by and by the mission station where this good man but poor bookkeeper had once lived reached out into adjoining fields and sent missionaries into the section where this man had gone unaided and alone. One missionary began to tell the people the story of Jesus, how he was the poor man's friend, how he loved little children, how he healed the sick, and to his surprise the people seemed to understand at once. Their faces were aglow, then one of them spoke and said, "Sahib, we know this man of whom you tell us. He has been living here for years." Amazed, the missionary then discovered that it was the man who had been dismissed by the Home Board because of his poor bookkeeping, who had come into that section and lived among the people, visiting them in their sickness, ministering to them in their times of need, incarnating the very spirit of Christ. Perhaps this particular missionary was not even up to the average in ability, but in fidelity a star of the first magnitude.

Faithfulness is a virtue; fidelity a grace; simple goodness a Christlike quality.

What has Christianity to offer to the average man? A goodly comradeship, the wonders of worship, the example of Christ? Yes, all of these, but chiefly a dynamic Gospel and a world objective. And the average man needs this. It is easy for him to become provincial and narrow in his

84

outlook. The average human life is chock full of difficulties. Many things combine to constrict and narrow the average man's vision. Christianity supplies a world view, a universal Gospel, an ample program, a noble idea of God, and an exalted view of man. James Boswell, the inimitable biographer of Samuel Johnson, describes Wilberforce, the British statesman, as he once heard him in a public address. Wilberforce was a very small man physically, almost a dwarf, and when he appeared to make his speech Boswell remarked that a shrimp had mounted the platform. Wilberforce was the champion of the slaves and their freedom, and as he warmed up to his subject he seemed to expand and his slight figure grew so that Boswell exclaimed, "Lo, the shrimp became a whale."

Now the teaching of Christ, his global-mindedness, and the world objectives of his gospel are designed to emancipate us from the tyranny of littleness, enlarge our vision, and make us spiritual cosmopolites. Moreover, rightly interpreted, the program of Christ appeals to the heroic, that splendid quality that slumbers in almost every man. The founder of the Christian religion believed there was a hero in the soul of the average man and acted upon that belief. His followers cannot do less than try to match their Master's spirit in this respect and emulate his sturdy confidence in the rank and file.

Can the average church appeal successfully to the average man? That depends. If the church has become institutionalized, bereft of spiritual charm, and in bondage to outworn and discredited methods, the average man will pass it by and find his inspirations and comradeships elsewhere. The old proverb that a new broom sweeps clean is fraught with wisdom. The first-century church met exigencies as they emerged and adopted methods suitable to the time and the need. Where there is spiritual vitality and intelligent leadership methods, policies, programs follow in due season.

But the churches will have to supply something better than mere physical comforts, dinners, athletics, clubs. These are by-products, incidentals—the average man yearns for something deeper, higher, more vital. He waits for the marks of the great fellowship. Show him these, make him feel the splendor and warmth of such a communion of spirits, and he will acknowledge the priority of the church, but not before.

It is foolish to belittle or ignore leadership. Ability to lead must command respect always. Nevertheless, leaders are useless unless they win a following. Generals, colonels, captains, bosses, foremen, superintendents, bishops, they have their reward, but what about the private, the men and women in the ranks, the workers in the fields, the ditches, and the streets, the housekeepers, and the army of toilers?

Occasionally the privates speak out in meetings. The state of Mississippi used to have a representative in Congress from the town of Tupelo who was a wit and a wag, by name, "Private" John Allen. He gloried in this term "Private" and it served him well. He was opposed for the nomination at a primary election by a general of some renown. The campaign opened with a joint debate and the general spoke first. In substance he said, "Fellow citizens, as you know, I served the Confederacy as a commanding officer. I had my full share in hardships, sufferings on the field of battle. I recall one night when a terrific storm broke over the headquarters my tent was deluged with rain and leaked badly. I got up, and there was an inch or two of water on the floor of the tent. Looking out through

86

the flap, I saw a sentry pacing to and fro in the rain. Back and forth he paced through the mud, and as I stood there the rain blew in on me in gusts. I was damp and cold and uncomfortable. I gave what I had to a noble cause. I think I earned your support. You should send me to Congress." Amidst applause the general sat down.

Private John Allen arose, advanced to the front of the platform, and when the handclapping had subsided, rejoined, "Fellow citizens, I was that sentry out in the rain, the sentry sloshing through the mud—I was that man. Now all of you who were generals in the late unpleasantness vote for my opponent, and all who were privates vote for mè." The general "also ran."

Thomas Carlyle once wrote something about the masses in which he alluded to them as "the plurality of blockheads." "Tammas" must have had a twinge of dyspepsia when he coined that ugly phrase. Jesus never said anything like that and his patience with his twelve friends recruited from the people, though often taxed, never flagged. No wonder the common people heard him gladly.

It is good to remember that not so many years ago there was among us, and sprung from lowly beginnings, one whom Tolstoy called "a miniature Christ." Once upon a time this son of poverty who bore unimagined burdens of state remarked, "You can fool all the people some of the time and some of the people all the time, but you can't fool all the people all the time."

The GOSPEL of "WE"

Colonel Charles A. Lindbergh gave a new meaning to the personal pronoun, first person plural. He identified himself with the ship that took him on his famous trip across the Atlantic. "We did it," he said, "the ship and I." This "we" spirit is essential to Christianity, fundamental in democracy, vital to the home. It is the "we" section of the Book of Acts that takes on a livelier color and an added thrill.

VIII

The sixteenth chapter of Acts is an arresting narrative. It contains the vision of the man of Macedonia, which turned out to be a woman. It chronicles also the dramatic account of Paul and Silas in prison with their feet in stocks, but singing hymns and praising God at midnight. Yet this chapter is not especially noted because of these features, interesting as they are.

The "We" section of Acts begins with this tenth verse of the sixteenth chapter. Hitherto the author has written in the third person, but at this point he joins St. Paul and becomes part of what he writes. From now on for the greater part of the story the historian writes as an observer and a sharer, and the narrative is the more pictorial and thrilling for this reason.

It was Colonel Charles A. Lindbergh who gave a new meaning to the personal pronoun, first person plural. He speaks of his achievement in flying from New York to Paris as a partnership affair. "We did it," he says, by which he means, I suppose, not only his plane and himself, but also his mother, the memory of his father, and myriad influences that contributed to an event that captured the imagination of the world and gave that young flying eagle a place in the sun. Fittingly, Colonel Lindbergh called his book *We*. No other title could possibly be so appropriate.

It is possible to appraise character by the personal pronouns one uses. There is an assertive "I" that is centered in self. There is an egotistic view of life and of self that is arrogantly expressed in the perpendicular pronoun. I remember hearing Mr. Bryan say that most men who prided themselves as self-made men worshiped their maker. There is an Old Testament character who illustrates the selfish, conceited, egotist whose world begins and ends in himself—Nebuchadnezzar, by name, king of Babylon. This haughty despot had a habit of striding along the walls of Babylon, looking about him in a supercilious fashion and exclaiming, "Is not this great Babylon which I built for the royal dwelling-place, by the might of my power, and for the glory of my majesty?" In that proud boast the king forgot the hordes of slaves that had carried the stones and timbers, the men that had borne the burden of the day and whose unrequited toils had made possible the splendid city; he forgot his loyal subjects, his friends and acquaintances, the members of his family; he forgot God. He remembered only himself as the builder of the city, and from that proud eminence of power and splendor this king who said "I" and "me" and "mine" was reduced to the lowliest of states and ate grass like a beast of the field.

There is another character correctly typified by the pronoun "they." This is a type diametrically different from the arrogant, assertive individual who thinks and speaks and writes in the terms of "I." This is a detached view of life, that expresses itself as one on the side lines, an observer, an onlooker. "They" do this and that. "They" run the government, "they" direct the church affairs, "they" are responsible, "they" are to blame. There is a college in Edinburgh which has over the doorway this inscription: "They say. What do they say? Let them say."

How both of these types suffer, the "I" and "they" views of life, as compared with the "we" spirit, which means cooperation, sharing, togetherness. The firm, "I, you, and they," may promise much in the beginning, but disaster will overtake and dissolve that firm sooner or later. The old-fashioned house of "We, us, and company" is bound to succeed because it is based on brotherhood and the idea of comity, comradeship, and teamwork.

This "we" spirit is fundamental in a democracy. "We, the people"—is one of the immortal phrases in the Declaration of Independence. It was a certain king who made bold to say, "I am the state." Democracy teaches us to say, "We are the state." The history of this Republic, the story of its beginnings, is shot through and through with this "we" principle, this idea of distributing responsibility and working together toward a common goal.

What is more informative or inspiring than the annals of the Constitutional Convention? Through long weary days and an unusually hot summer the representatives from the various states discussed, controverted, debated, various items and paragraphs of the rough draft of a document designed to hold together a number of states in one indivisible union. General George Washington was chosen president of that convention. He assumed the responsibility seriously, and during those numerous sessions and wearisome debates he presided with gravity and dignity. He must have been greatly bored, his heart was at Mt. Vernon with his beloved outdoor life, his flocks and herds, but his countrymen had imposed upon him responsibility and he could not refuse. So day after day Washington forgot his personal interests and natural desires, and remembered only the young nation and its solemn obligations of citizenship.

Different types of minds were represented in that convention. At one extreme, Alexander Hamilton; at another, James Madison, who reflected the view of Thomas Jefferson. Speech followed speech. There were omissions from the original draft and changes of phrasings, whole sections were omitted or drastically revised. Then came a day when Alexander Hamilton arose and said that while the Constitution did not suit him in some respects, yet he was willing to accept it as a whole. And James Madison expressed himself as not satisfied with some particulars of the document, but that he was ready to approve it in the interests of harmony and unity. And so the "We" spirit entered vitally into the beginnings of our nation, and our institutions can only be preserved and perpetuated healthfully by a continuation of this same spirit of give and take, of willingness to share and coöperate in the affairs of state.

It is the "we" spirit in the home that preserves the family. The family is a republic within a republic. Where there is a spirit of sharing responsibility and privilege in the home and proper consideration shown each member of the family group, the result is a strength and a unity that can withstand any vicissitude or disaster.

Once I put up at a resort hotel where the partition between the rooms was not sound-proof. Two ladies came in the room adjoining mine. I had no wish to eavesdrop, but I could not help overhearing their conversation. My neighbors were, I judged, two girls, and their conversation was about young men, strange to say. One had a cool soprano voice and the other a rich contralto. The soprano asked the contralto's opinion of a certain young man and what she thought of him. She replied, "He is the most charmingly naïve creature I ever met." Then the soprano made inquiry of another. "As for him," replied the contralto, "he is the most boring young fellow I ever knew." And so the conversation went on, and at last there appeared in the conversation a young man that the contralto thought was exactly right, and the soprano seemed greatly interested and pleased to know this.

Imagine my surprise when I discovered that the occupants of the room adjoining me were mother and daughter. I saw them frequently after that in the dining-room, and no two girls, even the closest chums, could have been more interested in each other than that mother and daughter. I thought it was ideal for a mother and daughter to be so delightfully and intimately interested in such a subject. And I fancied that that daughter's marriage was not likely to be a failure, and that even if it should be that there was such an understanding between that mother and daughter, something could be salvaged even from matrimonial shipwreck. This "we" spirit in the home is the guardian of the highest interests of the family, whereas the "I" and the "they" spirit crassly expressing itself in the family group means discord, disappointment and destruction.

The "we" spirit is the very essence of Christianity. It takes at least two people to practice the teachings of Christ.

Jesus said that love to God and love to one's neighbor was the summing up of all the law and the prophets. He announced that "where two or three are gathered together in my name there am I in the midst." Notice that the lowest number is two, that it takes at least yourself and somebody else and God to form this trinity. When Jesus sent his disciples out he sent them two by two. Thus we have again exemplified the "we" spirit.

Interesting, too, is the fact that Jesus associated himself with God. His ministry was a sharing and an association with the heavenly Father. He said: "My Father worketh hitherto and I work"; "The Father is greater than I"; "I and the Father are one." He enjoyed this unbroken sense of God's presence. He never thought of himself alone, even when no human companion was near. God was with him. Jesus identified himself with his followers. "Lo, I am with you always, even unto the end of the world."

The great hearts of the world, the prophetic souls that have led unpopular movements and championed the cause of the long wronged, have had an abiding sense of the comradeship of the Unseen. They were "we" men who reckoned with God. Cromwell had it. Lincoln possessed it. In the darkest hours of the Civil War, when the heart of Lincoln was bowed with anxiety and grief, he had a realization that God was with him. He sensed His presence and was comforted and encouraged thereby. Woodrow Wilson had it. Broken and defeated, he rested his case on the sovereignty of God and the "slow years." St. Paul felt it. In the shipwreck and the storm he perceived the presence of the Invisible and averred that God stood by him. It is this companionship of the Unseen which fortifies the grief-laden and buttresses the weary-hearted in every walk of life. Faith itself is, when most simply defined, the sensing of the presence of God, the sweet assurance that one is not fighting single-handed the battles of life. It is this "we" spirit in every aspect of life, that ennobles, and makes the bitterest and most difficult experiences not only endurable, but also fruitfully rewarding.

> "But when ye pray, say our—not mine or thine:
> Our debts, our debtors, and our daily bread!
> Before the thronged cathedral's gracious shrine,
> Or in thy closet's solitude instead,
> Whoe'er thou art, where'er thou liftest prayer,
> However humble or how great thou be,
> Say our, thy brother man including there,
> And more and more it may be thou shalt see
> Upon life's loom how thread to thread is bound;
> None for himself, but man and fellow-man,
> Or near or far, meet on one common ground,
> Sons of one Father since the world began.
> So shall God's Kingdom come in might and power
> When all can pray, not mine, or thine, but our."

ROSES of BETHANY or LILIES of ARIMATHEA?

One sentence in that famous letter of old Doctor Johnson to Lord Chesterfield deserves to be printed in some striking form, framed and hung in a conspicuous place. It is this: "The notice which you have been pleased to take of my labors, had it been early, had been kind; but it has been delayed till I am indifferent, and cannot enjoy it; till I am known and do not want it." No paradox of the New Testament is more arresting than the story of Mary's gift to the living Jesus and the ministry of Joseph of Arimathea to the dead Nazarene.

IX

8396

ROSES

"Now when Jesus was in Bethany, in the house of Simon the leper, there came unto him a woman having an alabaster cruse of exceeding precious ointment, and she poured it upon his head, as he sat at meat. But when the disciples saw it, they had indignation, saying, To what purpose is this waste? For this ointment might have been sold for much, and given to the poor. But Jesus perceiving it said unto them, Why trouble ye the woman? for she hath wrought a good work upon me. For ye have the poor always with you; but me ye have not always. For in that she poured this ointment upon my body, she did it to prepare me for burial. Verily I say unto you, Wheresoever this gospel shall be preached in the whole world, that also which this woman hath done shall be spoken of for a memorial of her."

Matthew XXVI:13

LILIES

"And when even was now come, because it was the Preparation, that is, the day before the Sabbath, there came Joseph of Arimathea, a councillor of honorable estate, who also himself was looking for the kingdom of God; and he boldly went in unto Pilate, and asked for the body of Jesus. And Pilate marvelled if he were already dead: and calling unto him the centurion, he asked him whether he had been any while dead. And when he learned it of the centurion, he granted the corpse to Joseph. And he bought a linen cloth, and taking him down, wound him in the linen cloth, and laid him in a tomb which had been hewn out of a rock; and he rolled a stone against the door of the tomb."

Mark XV:42-46

The last week of Jesus of Nazareth was marked by paradoxes; joyous surprises, bitter disappointments. Curious contrasts waited one upon another. Vicissitudes strangely unlike followed hard and fast. Lights and shadows intermingled. It was a holy week, yet marred by unholy episodes.

A striking paradox of that week was the kiss of Judas and the deed of Pilate's wife. One of Jesus' disciples bargained with his enemies to deliver him into their hands and sealed the sordid business with a kiss. Such conduct is difficult to explain. There is something serpentine about a traitor, something devilish about treason. The betrayal at the hands of Judas was a more painful ordeal for Jesus than the spitting in his face, the mockery by Herod's soldiers, or the indecent choice of Barabbas by the rabble.

Alongside of this strange and wicked deed a Roman woman, the wife of Pontius Pilate, governor of the province, interceded with her husband to save Jesus from the cross. It is unlikely that she had met or talked with him, perchance only glimpsed him from her latticed window, or maybe she had heard the story of his wondrous deeds from some servant in her household. However, this may have been, her heart was filled with a vast pity for Jesus and she did what she could in his behalf. She wrote a little note to her husband, beseeching him to be considerate of his unusual prisoner and to spare him pain. The act was wholly unexpected, and one may believe without a precedent. It did credit to the goodness of this Roman matron's heart and her womanly intuition. The deed helped to assuage the blow of Judas, struck in the dark and under cover of a sign of friendship.

A second paradox was the defection of the Twelve and the confession of the centurion. Jesus' disciples deserted him in his utmost need. There is no more pathetic verse in all the Scripture than this, "They all forsook him and fled." Even Simon Peter, who boasted he would stand by his Master if all the others forsook him, took to his heels. Thomas the loyal slunk away, and John, "the disciple whom Jesus loved," was numbered among the deserters.

Over against this unlovely picture of the defection of the band of disciples is that of a Roman officer, the captain in charge of the guard which was on duty at the crucifixion. And such a picture it is! This centurion, accustomed to scenes of bloodshed and human woe, was deeply stirred as he surveyed that central cross. He observed the dying Nazarene as he provided a home for his mother; listened as he forgave the penitent robber; heard in amazement his prayer for his enemies; and when at last Jesus died with a loud cry on his parched lips the centurion, profoundly moved, exclaimed, "Truly this was the Son of God." Now, whatever the Roman officer meant by these words, his tribute was as noble as it was surprising. With the twelve intimates scattered as so many sheep abandoning the shepherd to his doom, that grim soldierly figure standing in front of the cross, a spirit of reverence filling his being and an affirmation of homage on his lips, is a heartening spectacle. It helps to relieve the tensity of the scene, it shines like the glimmer of a star on a dark and stormy night.

A third paradox was the sword of Peter unsheathed against the enemies of Jesus and the prayer of Jesus from the cross in behalf of those who nailed him there. What a contrast in attitude of mind and emotions; the impetuous disciple stirred to anger, wielding the sword and shedding blood; the serene Master praying, "Father, forgive them for they know not what they do." The weapon of this world and the sword of the Spirit; the eye-for-an-eye doctrine *versus* the practice of the "second-mile" teaching. A startling paradox, is it not?

Yet, arresting as these contrasts are, there is a fourth more arresting still. Two friends of Jesus, a devout woman of Bethany and a wealthy citizen of Jerusalem, were the leading characters in the episode of roses of Bethany and lilies of Arimathea.

Jesus was a dinner guest in the house of Simon of Bethany. Lazarus, Mary, Martha, and the twelve disciples were honored guests. At an appropriate moment Mary appeared with an alabaster flask filled with a rare and costly perfume. She probably attempted to loosen the stopper, but, failing in this and in the abandon of her affection for Jesus she broke the neck of the flask and poured its precious contents in a fragrant stream over his head so that it ran down his body, dripped upon his feet, and the room was as fragrant as the perfumed breezes that blow from off an apple orchard in blossom time.

But critics were present. Judas was not pleased with what had occurred. He spoke out boldly. "Why was not this perfume sold and the price given to the poor?" he scolded. A murmur of disapproval of Mary's deed passed among the guests as incongruous as a cold wind blowing across a rose garden in June. Then Jesus administered a strong rebuke to the detractors of Mary's deed, followed by high praise for Mary. "Why trouble ye her? She hath wrought a good work upon me, for in that she hath poured this ointment on my body, she did it for my burial. Verily I say unto you, wheresoever the gospel shall be preached

104

throughout the whole world, this also that she hath done shall be spoken of for a memorial of her."

Mary's gracious deed I love to think of as a cluster of roses given her Master while he could feast his eyes on their beauty and breathe deep their fragrance. What an exquisitely beautiful thing Mary did that day for Jesus' sake! Nothing could have been more appropriate, nor anything else quite so perfect as this deed performed a few days before the billows of hate beat against Jesus and bore him to the cross. It was the roses of Bethany that helped Jesus to bear the thorns of Jerusalem so soon to pierce his flesh. It was characteristic of him to reprimand her critics and praise the author of such a gracious and tender ministry.

The thing that clothes Mary's ministry with splendor is the fact that it had apparently no practical purpose. It seemed, in the eyes of cold, hard-headed men, extravagant, wasteful, and unnecessary. Yet such deeds, courteous, thoughtful, costly, contribute to life something fine and cultural. They are the extras that make life worth living and without which the days would be drab and dreary. To the stolid, the undiscerning, and the censorious, gifts such as Mary's are foolish, wasteful, impractical, but to others who live in their affections such offerings are tender, inspiring, full of sentiment, deathless.

In a mid-western city there lived for many years the widowed mother of one of the successful business men of America. The son, residing five hundred miles distant, through a period of twenty years sent on Saturday of every week a gift of flowers to his mother. Week after week they came, roses, carnations, violets, sweet peas, orchids, fresh, fragrant, lovely. I estimate that through those years the cost of the weekly gift of flowers was three thousand dollars or more. Was it an extravagance? Is a love gift ever extravagant? Many a time I have been a guest in that home when a glad-eyed woman, upon whom the infirmities of age were stealing, proudly asked me to look at her flowers, the weekly token of her son's solicitous affection. There was a mother who had her roses when they meant most to her; she prized them, they filled her life with love and peace. And when she went the way of all the earth the flowers that filled the room where she lay in the dignity of death were not the empty mockery they sometimes seem when too long delayed.

When my gifted friend Joseph Fort Newton went from a church in Cedar Rapids, Iowa, to become minister of the famous City Temple, London, he did a venturesome thing. Under the most favorable conditions an American preacher in the British Isles is often a lonely creature. At the time Dr. Newton began his London ministry this country had not yet gone into the Great War and the relations between the two countries were a little strained. As the time drew near for Dr. Newton to go into the pulpit that first Sunday he felt singularly depressed and a wave of homesickness swept over him. Then it was that an office bearer brought into the vestry a great cluster of American Beauty roses, and with the flowers was a cheery little note assuring Dr. Newton that the congregation were remembering him in grateful prayer. Dr. Newton's drooping spirits were revived magically. He felt renewed in mind and body. He rose grandly to the occasion and spoke with prophetic unction. Roses of Bethany! What good medicine within their petals! What gift of healing in their perfume!

In the zenith of Dr. Newell Dwight Hillis' fame as minister of Plymouth Church, Brooklyn, he lectured in a small Indiana city. He was the guest of the pastor of a small church, a young man who was fighting a hard battle against heavy odds. It happened that Dr. Hillis was in the young preacher's study, and, left by himself, glanced at the small but carefully selected library. Observing one of his own books on the topmost shelf, he took it down, and on the fly-leaf the renowned Brooklyn preacher wrote a sentiment, personal and tender, signed his name, and returned the book to its place. Some weeks later the young preacher happened to discover the inscription and was overjoyed. It greatly gentled and inspired him, put hope in his heart, a new purpose in his ministry. A little thing, you say? Nay, a great thing, beautiful, eloquent, a modern instance of roses of Bethany just when their beauty and fragrance meant the most.

In a city of the corn belt of Illinois a family of fine old-fashioned ideals brought up to a noble maturity a splendid company of sons and daughters. For the most part the children married in the community and settled down there, establishing homes after the same ample pattern of their parents. From the first of their wedded lives these young people formed the habit of gathering every Sunday evening in the old home for a light meal together and a joyous family reunion, and the gay and wholesome conversation that glorifies such occasions. As the grandchildren came they were brought along, and the custom continued long after both of the parents had been taken by death. This custom cost the younger generation some sacrifices and inconveniences, but it repaid the family in countless ways. It imparted splendor to the family life and gave it solidarity.

Roses of Bethany, flowers for the living, ministries that heal and bless while the struggle of life is on, burdens weigh heavily and middle age glides into time of sunset and evening star. Roses, roses, red roses of Bethany!

Joseph of Arimathea was evidently a prominent citizen of Jerusalem, wealthy and influential. He was a member of the Jewish council, or Sanhedrin, a man of high standing, reputable, a chief citizen. He was more than an admirer of Jesus; he had come to be his disciple, but not openly. He was a secret disciple for fear of the Jews, according to John. There is something pathetic in this comment, and not altogether creditable to Joseph. Here was a man of high social and business standing, interested in a religious teacher who was of the common people, whose strong indictment of the religious leaders of his day had made him a heretic and a rebel. Joseph of Arimathea could not get the consent of his will to step boldly out and take his stand publicly as a disciple of Jesus. Let us believe that he struggled to overcome this fear. It was a severe test and Joseph failed to meet it.

It is not difficult to imagine how Joseph must have suffered when he saw Jesus led through the streets of Jerusalem, on his way to die the death of a common felon. Picture him looking out from his sheltered room, watching the pitiful procession and Jesus staggering beneath the burden of the cross. Hear him in anguish say to himself, "Oh, that I had the courage to go out now and stand by him, to brave all the taunts of all Jerusalem and help him bear his cross, and cheer him along the sorrowful way!" But, no; Joseph could not bring himself to go to Jesus' aid. The procession passed and Joseph of Arimathea was still a secret disciple of Jesus. . . . The heart of the chief citizen of Jerusalem was with the Saviour as he went to his death, but he walked not by his side, nor raised his voice in Jesus' behalf.

The supreme tragedy moved on apace. The agony of the cross was at an end. After six hours of pain and suffering Jesus died, saying, "Father, into thy hands I commend my spirit." The multitude scattered; the weeping women withdrew; the saddest of days drew to its close. Then, and not until then, Joseph of Arimathea came out into the open. Boldly he went to Pilate and asked for the body of Jesus that he might give it a decent burial. The Roman governor acceded to his request, and he who had hesitated to associate himself with Jesus in life became identified with him in death. The portraits that show the descent of Jesus from the cross, particularly that of Ruben's are worthy anyone's study. Gently, tenderly, they took down the body, and decently composed it for burial. Joseph of Arimathea carefully supervised the necessary preparations for entombment. Nothing was too good for the lifeless form. The finest of linen was wrapped about the body, and costly balm and myrrh plentifully used. Thus in Joseph's new tomb, where no body had rested, Jesus was given the burial of the rich and great.

I would not belittle this ministry of Joseph of Arimathea, nor overlook his solicitude for the dead body of Jesus. It is not without its practical side, nor is it devoid of sentiment. It cost Joseph something to do this deed. To brave the criticism of his fellow citizens even at so late an hour called for courage. But this deed suffers when compared with Mary's fragrant deed. It came too late to accomplish the greatest good. White lilies of Arimathea are beautiful, but not nearly so lovely as red, red roses of Bethany.

Ponder these short incisive lines by a modern poet inscribed "To Joseph of Arimathea":

"Strange quiet man, what impulse in your breast
 Invoked your kindness to the Master whom
You had not dared to join? He wanted rest
 Within your heart, but found it in your tomb.
Did you not dare to love him, he who sought
 To give you life, nor asked for recompense?
What pity that in finding him you brought
 Your laggard love in death's cold cerements!"[1]

At the north side of Cass Park, Detroit, is a statue of
Robert Burns. It is a fine piece of bronze and attracts the
attention of many a passer-by. It stands on a pedestal on
the four sides of which are pictured scenes from "Tam o'
Shanter" and "The Cotter's Saturday Night." Following
the annual birthday of Scotland's famous son, gorgeous
flowers, costly garlands, and flaming wreaths, are heaped
lavishly about this statue. More than once I have stopped
and mused awhile before this bronze figure with the flowers heaped at its base. I have thought how the poet suffered in life, how shabbily he was treated even by those
who should have known better and for whom excuses are
difficult to find. I recalled the poet's poverty, the pitiful-
ness of it all, and I have said, "Robert Burns has now his
lilies of Arimathea, but, oh, that red roses of Bethany
might have been his, when the sight of them would have
gladdened the eyes of that dear singer who sang, 'My
luve is like a red, red rose,' and their perfume thrilled his
sensitive soul."

I have been attending Lincoln celebrations for many
years and am accustomed to hear the great Kentuckian
eulogized and praised to the skies. Such homage is due one
of the supreme figures of all times, yet when I hear eloquent
speakers lavish encomiums on Abraham Lincoln I recall

---

[1] Quoted by permission of the *Christian Century*.

how few roses he had in his lifetime. He was never a popular hero in the days of his flesh. I recall that when the "bronzed, lank man, prairie lawyer, master of us all," was bearing the colossal burden of state a partisan arose in the Congress and said, "You might search hell over and find no more miserable wretch than Abraham Lincoln." Would that the "captain of the mighty heart" might have had a little of the praise during his lifetime that we heap upon his memory now that he has gone from among us.

During the World War an American President dreamed a great dream of the nations of the world leagued together to further the cause of peace on earth and good will among men. In ardent sincerity this man, when there seemed no other solution, led us into a war to end war, ever keeping in mind the idea of an international agreement for world peace. The aftermath of the world conflict involved him in controversy, broke him physically, and brought upon his head an avalanche of detraction and bitter criticism such as happened to no other American President save Lincoln. He went to his death a victim of the war as truly as any soldier who fell on Flander's field. After "the great teacher's death" had brought peace to this prophet of a better day, eulogies fell from the lips of those who had bitterly assailed him in life. Editorials praised him to the skies and the nation wept by his coffin. Would that he had had some of these roses when the days were long and the way was bitter. Would that some of this praise might have been spoken when Woodrow Wilson was here in the flesh, bearing his herculean burden of state, engulfed by all the hates of war released by disillusionment and the war weariness that followed the Armistice.

In an Eastern city, an able and hard-working minister decided, after a struggle, to resign from the church to which he had ministered for a decade, and accept another pastorate in a distant state. There was no particular reason for his leaving save a feeling that there was no great demand for his remaining. The church was in excellent condition, he had a constructive program, yet somehow he was not sure that the sentiment for his remaining was strong enough to justify it. After heartache and struggle he resigned. He read his resignation at a Sunday service and there followed a great demonstration of esteem and affection. The next day one of the most influential members of the congregation, a man naturally reserved and distant, called to see him. To the minister's surprise his visitor had come to tell him how much his sermons had meant to him, instancing one in particular which had profoundly affected his life. The minister listened with amazement till his visitor had finished, then he said: "Why didn't you let me know this before? Why didn't you talk like this to me a week ago? If you had done so it might have helped me to a different decision." The man of business was silent for a time, then he said: "I don't know. I suppose I took it for granted that you understood, or maybe I just forgot it. Anyway I can't think of an excuse. I'm dreadfully sorry."

Old Doctor Samuel Johnson understood the meaning of lilies of Arimathea. How well he knew the futility of a kindness done too late is mirrored in his famous letter to Lord Chesterfield when that nobleman took a tardy notice of Johnson's monumental work, a Dictionary of the English Language. The old doctor's letter, his opinion of a belated service, is phrased in marvelous English.

"Seven years, my lord, have now passed since I waited in your outward rooms, or was repulsed from your door; during which time I have been pushing on my work through difficulties, of which it is useless to complain, and have brought it, at last, to the verge of publication, without one act of assistance, one word of encouragement, or one smile of favor. Such treatment I did not expect, for I never had a patron before. . . . The notice which you have been pleased to take of my labors, had it been early, had been kind; but it has been delayed till I am indifferent, and cannot enjoy it; till I am known and do not want it. I hope it is no cynical asperity, not to confess obligations when no benefit has been received, or to be unwilling that the public should consider me as owing that to a patron which Providence has enabled me to do for myself."

Belated kindnesses, neglected offices of sympathy, postponed ministries that might have healed and blessed—how their memories haunt and trouble us! There is nothing new in this theme. It is as old as humanity. Certain as we are of change and inevitable as we know death to be, we neglect and postpone the most beautiful services of life. It costs so little to be kind, means so much to be considerate, is so Christlike to forgive.

Jesus magnified life and minimized death. Too often we reverse this order, are strangely forgetful in the midst of life, and when death and disaster come to those about us seek to offset our sins of omission by opulent offerings brought too late to accomplish the greatest good. Abraham Lincoln never wrote anything more revealing or more practical than the sentiment which he set down in a letter to his dear friend Joshua Speed: "Speed, die when I may, I want it said of me by those who knew me best that I always plucked a thistle and planted a flower where a flower would grow."

Already there are too many organizations, orders, fraternities, in this modern world of ours, but I am minded to suggest one more, namely, Pluckers of Thistles and Planters of Roses—Roses of Bethany!

THANK GOD—and REPENT

Of all our national holidays, Thanksgiving Day is rainbowed with the glory of a deep religious spirit. The fragrance of the Book of Psalms clings to the day and institution as the scent of roses clings to a vase. It is an appropriate season to take a spiritual as well as a material inventory, a time to thank God—and repent.

X

In the annual proclamation of the President of the United States occurs this felicitous phrase: "Thanksgiving Day is the most characteristic of our national observances." It is this and more—it is the most widely observed and the most predominantly religious of all our national celebrations. More than any other of our holidays, Thanksgiving has retained to a marked degree its original luster. Independence Day has suffered at the hands of political promoters and the flamboyant proclamation of a narrow nationalism. Likewise, the Christmas festival has sustained loss, and much merchandising has dimmed its spiritual glow. The birthday of Washington finds no general observance such as it deserves. But the celebration of Thanksgiving Day is known and kept in some form or other all the way from the crowded metropolis to the remotest farmhouse. There is a certain mellowness in the day, a something fine and ennobling.

The first text of Scripture I have selected is from the farewell address attributed to Moses and is as appropriate for this day as it is impressive in tone. "The tongues of dying men enforce attention like deep harmony" and the dominant note in this Scripture is gratitude for divine guidance in the past and deep solicitude for the future. In sober, almost pathetic speech the children of Israel are counseled not to forget the past and bidden to tell the story of the benignant Providence that prospered them all along the way. Thanksgiving Day in this year of our Lord is the time to remember the days of old in order to fulfill in the new days the high hopes and aspirations of our holy faith.

This is a day of mystic memories of our nation's glorious youth. Youthful years are rainbowed with poetry and romance always. The high venturesomeness, the buoyancy, the dreams and visions, the sheer joy of living—these characterize and belong to youth, even the youth of a nation. The story of the settlement along New England's shores by the Pilgrims is more than a thrice-told tale, but never a threadbare theme. Mrs. Hemans is a minor poet, but she struck a lofty strain in her "Landing of the Pilgrim Fathers." The meter, the phrases, the figures—all are in perfect accord with the theme. Her lines capture the imagination, and particularly fine are these stanzas:

> "Amidst the storm they sang
> And the stars heard, and the sea,
> And the sounding aisles of the dim wood rang
> To the anthem of the free.

> "And the ocean eagle soared
> From his nest by the white wave's foam,
> And the rocking pines of the forest roared—
> This, was their welcome home."

This is not soft music—this is organ note—this is fortissimo, a kind of hallelujah chorus. Oh, pioneers, star-eyed, brave-hearted, God-fearing, heroic men and women, how great our need for your faith, your fortitude, your willingness to endure hardship!

There is a picture of the Pilgrims on their way to church which has been copied so often and circulated so widely that almost every schoolboy has seen it. The little company has set out for the meeting-house—men, women, and children. The minister and his wife walk side by side, he carrying a copy of the Holy Scriptures. The men, wearing high-crowned hats and arrayed in their Sunday best, bear arms and are on the watchout for some lurking enemy in ambush. It is in the dead of winter and snow is on the ground. In the background is the forest and at the edge the few houses of the settlement. It may not be a great picture, according to artistic standards, but there is upon it such a light as never was on sea or land—demure maidens, sedate matrons, competent and fearless husbands and sons, a goodly company, and as you look at the picture you can only feel that their trust is not so much in the firearms which they carry as the God "beneath whose guiding hand our exiled Fathers crossed the sea."

This is a day of grateful and exultant praise to the heavenly Father for His bounties. The gratitude of the Colonists that bleak December of 1621 was expressed with abandon and deepest sincerity. They thanked God for the rather meager crops that were theirs and praised Him unstintedly for the wondrous way in which they had been led. When we recall how few their numbers, how far they were from their motherland and that they were encircled by perils both known and unknown, we can but marvel because of their simple faith, their grateful hearts and high courage. How myriad are the blessings that are ours, even after the fullest deductions have been made for loss, separation, grief, and disappointments.

Let us thank God for His bounties. We cannot number His mercies. They are as the sands which by the sea shore are innumerable. The Psalmist attempts to enumerate these blessings and is bewildered by the opulence that besets him behind and before. Embarrassed, but still articulate, he exclaims, "Let everything that hath breath praise the Lord." Suppose we try to take stock: there is the wonder of His out-of-doors, the glory of the sunrise and the beauty of the sunset, the long wash of the surf on the beach, the majesty of mountain and the poetry of prairie, the vagrant flowers of the roadside and the cultivated creations that glorify the gardens, and the lordly trees of forest and woodland pastures, the marvel of the heavens with their multitudinous stars, the witchery of shining moon. God be praised for this world in which we live with its colors and mysteries, scents and sounds.

"Ask for what end the heavenly bodies shine,
Earth for whose use? Pride answers, ' 'Tis for mine;
For me kind nature wakes her genial power,
Suckles each herb, and spreads out every flower;
Annual for me, the grape, the rose, renew
The juice nectareous and the balmy dew;
For me, the mine a thousand treasures brings;
For me, health gushes from a thousand springs;
Seas roll to waft me, suns to light me rise;
My footstool earth, my canopy the skies.' "

There are the flowers and fruits of friendship—have we not good reason to thank God for these? It was an American, H. Clay Trumbull, who wrote a widely read book entitled *Friendship—The Master Passion*. An English publication offered a prize for the best definition of a friend, and among the thousands of answers received were the following: "One who multiplies joys, divides grief, and whose honesty is inviolable." "One who understands our silence." "A volume of sympathy bound in cloth." "A watch which beats true for all time and never runs down." And here is the definition that won the prize—"A friend is the one who comes in when the whole world has gone out." Even as David thanked God for Jonathan and praised him in well-remembered lines, so have we abundant reasons to thank God today for friends and to resolve that we shall keep these friendships in constant repair.

There too are the joys and loves of family life, the tender and holy relations we bear and share in the home; for these, too, we thank God today. The debt we owe to husband, wife, father, mother, son, and daughter has found expression in numerous ways, and uniquely so in the dedicatory inscriptions authors place in their books. Thus General Lew Wallace dedicates *Ben-Hur*, his most famous work, "To the wife of my Youth Who Still Abides with Me." Henry van Dyke puts this sentiment on the fly-leaf of his *The Blue Flower*—"To the memory of Bernard van Dyke, 1887-1897, and the love that lives beyond the years." And only a heart of exquisite tenderness could so find voice as Professor Walter Rouschenbush in the dedication of his *Christianity and the Social Crisis*—"To the Women who have Loved me, My Mother, My Sisters Freida and Emma, My dear Wife Pauline, and my little daughters Winifred and Elizabeth."

Let us thank God for books; "The precious life-blood of a master spirit, embalmed and treasured on purpose to a life beyond life"; for pictures and that wide realm of art where every day may bring a fresh discovery or announce a new joy; for music, the ministry of melody, the world of haunting harmonies; for blessings such as these and myriad others unnamed, let our praises rise in glad halle-lujahs. Even the deep and dark experiences, the disap-pointments and defeats, the sorrows and separations—are they really such, or only apparently so? Have we not lived long enough to discover that what we call darkness and defeat but presaged light and victory? How incompetent we are to pass judgment upon the contemporary events or personal experiences of the day and hour. We are not yet able to see them in perspective, and until we may the lamp of faith must guide our feet.

And what abundant reason we have for gratitude be-cause of what has been done by the peacemakers since last we observed this day. Not since the World War ended has the prospect of peace been so bright and heartening as it is at this hour. Since 1918 the path of peace has been as the path of the just which is "as the shining light that shineth more and more unto the perfect day." Since then seven milestones have been set up along the way to peace on earth and good will among men. I have not the time to linger by each of these milestones. I but name them and let them speak for themselves.

The milestones are: (1) The League of Nations, 1920, with its fifty-five members among the nations of the earth, operative and making history. (2) The Disarmament Con-ference at Washington, 1921. A friendly gesture in which America showed her faith. (3) Locarno, 1925, where Mr. MacDonald and M. Herriot took advanced ground. (4) The World Conference of Christians at Stockholm, 1925, with thirty-seven nations represented and thirty-one com-munions participating. (5) The oversea flight in 1927 of Colonel Charles A. Lindbergh, the "Lone Eagle" who came like a good angel from the skies, a messenger of peace and good will to Europe and in 1928 to Mexico. (6) The Pact of Paris, 1928, when war was declared an outlaw and the greatest nations of the earth through their representatives affixed their signatures. (7) The recent friendly conference between President Hoover and Prime Minister Ramsay MacDonald, with its promise of far-reaching results. No Thanksgiving Day since 1913 is so freighted with reasons for rejoicing as Thanksgiving in the present year of our Lord.

I dare to dream a dream. It is the year 1969, and I see a veteran of the Great War, a member of the American Legion, holding on his knee his first great-grandchild. It is World Peace Day, the anniversary of the day when the last nation became a signatory of the treaty outlawing war. Flags are flying, bands of music are playing. I hear the little boy asking questions, a habit of little boys everywhere. "Grandad," he asks, toying with the old man's military medal, "were you really in the war, that last great war?" "Yes, my boy," the veteran replies. "It seems as a dream that men once fought one another like wild beasts, but it can never happen again, and some day you'll read the story how brave men and true fought the bloodless battles of peace. It was a long, hard fight, almost as hard as the fighting by land and sea where men suffered and died host upon host. A glorious company of heroic men, my boy, gave their lives pioneering for peace, and a like company of noble women went to early graves that peace on earth might come. It was not an easy victory." The veteran sighs, then smiles. "And will there be anything noble for me to do when I grow up, grandad?" "Aye, that there will, my boy. Work aplenty, and hard. The battles for justice, peace, and liberty are never finished. Every generation must serve this cause; and you will find a man's work awaiting you in behalf of the new world and the better day. But, boy, it's time to listen to the radio. There is a world hook-up and the President of the United States of Europe and our own President have something to tell the world." I dare to dream this dream today, thanking God for the progress of peace on earth and good will among men the while.

This is a day of contrition and penitence, as, indeed, every real Thanksgiving Day must be. Praise and penitence —they are twin graces of the truly religious. Reflecting on the blessings that have rained down upon us, these hearts of ours ought to be greatly gentled. Who of us can say he has done his best? Ugly pride, downright selfishness, silly prejudices, and childish intolerance, have marred our lives. The Scriptures admonish us that "a broken and a contrite heart" our God will not despise.

During the Great War a story appeared which attracted much attention. It was the story of a mother whose un-usually brilliant son gave his life on the field of battle. He was a genius and had flowered early. From youth up he had led his classes and won distinction at Oxford. He went to war and his life was blotted out instantly by an exploding shell. The mother dreamed a singular dream— she thought an angel appeared to her with the information that she might have her son back for five minutes. "Choose," said the angel, "what five minutes you will have. Will you have five minutes of his life when he was leading his classes at Oxford, or would you prefer to have five minutes of those days that he spent in the service of his country, those last days of his life?" The mother re-flected for a moment and said, "If I can have him back for just five minutes, I should prefer to have him, not as the

Oxford scholar, nor during his soldier days. If I can have him but five minutes, I want to have him as a little boy and on a day that he had disobeyed me. I remember how he ran into the garden, angry and rebellious, and then in a little while he came back and threw himself into my arms, asking me to forgive him. His face was hot and red; he looked so small and miserable and so precious, I saw his love in his eyes, I felt his love in his body pressed against my own, and how my love went out to him! If I can have him only five minutes, I want him back as that little penitent boy."

Is not this a parable for us? Is there any greater need than that of repentance among the nations and individuals? What have we today to tell our children of the days of old? And, what is more vital still, what will they have to tell their children of us? Will they be able to say that we fought a good fight—that we kept the simple faith in God and man—that we banished hate from our lives and began the rebuilding of a broken world on a new basis of brotherhood? How can we have comradeship with our fathers in the memory of an heroic past unless we have also a fellowship with them in deeds of sacrificial service for which our generation waits?

So let us thank God and repent. Thank Him for His many mercies, and repent of our shortcomings as a nation, as churches, as religious leaders and followers of the Christ. Let us repent of our foolish pride, exclusive spirit, snobbish ways. Let us repent of our partisanship, sectarianism, silly prejudices. Let us repent of our love of ease, creature comforts, sordid ambitions, passion for sheer achievements. Let us repent of our narrow nationalism, our parochial horizons, our provincial ideals. Let us repent of our extreme prudence, caution, and lack of adventuresomeness. Let us repent of the delusion that we need no repentance, and other self-deceptions that have subtracted from our higher usefulness. Let us repent and bring forth fruits worthy of repentance. Let us bring to Almighty God the sacrifice of an humble and a contrite heart on this day of old memories and of new dedications and resolutions.